D1499072

NOTES ON
THE LORD'S PRAYER

NOTES ON
THE LORD'S PRAYER

RAÏSSA MARITAIN

TRANSLATED FROM THE FRENCH

Foreword by THOMAS MERTON

Lord, teach us to pray
Luke 11: 1

P. J. KENEDY & SONS   NEW YORK

NOTES ON THE LORD'S PRAYER
is a translation of *Notes sur le Pater*
by Raïssa Maritain, originally published
by Desclée de Brouwer, Paris, France, 1962

Nihil obstat   Edward J. Montano, S.T.D.
            Censor Librorum
Imprimatur   ✠ FRANCIS CARDINAL SPELLMAN
            Archbishop of New York
New York, December 27, 1963

Library of Congress Catalog Card No. 64–13204
Copyright © 1964 by P. J. Kenedy & Sons
PRINTED IN THE UNITED STATES OF AMERICA

To the Little Brothers of Jesus

FOREWORD

Since the late Middle Ages there has developed a split between "spirituality" and "theology." The doctrine and experience of prayer have become the preserve of "devout persons" and mystics; theology in its turn has become a matter of technical expertise, essentially unconcerned with any spiritual experience or, indeed, with the interior life. Such at least is an observation that has frequently been made in recent years. This observation, though perhaps sometimes exaggerated, has not been without a basis in truth. Too often it has apparently been regarded as *normal* for the "spiritual writer" or "master of the spiritual life" to be quite distinct from, indeed alien to, the technical theologian. In reality, it is the opposite state of affairs that should be normal. "The theologian," said one of the Egyptian Fathers, "is the man of prayer, and the true man of prayer is the theologian." In saying this, Evagrius (in the *Sentences on Prayer* long ascribed to "St. Nilus") was simply saying that true theology embraces not only the speculative science of divine things but also an experiential wisdom of love which, by prayer, reaches beyond knowledge into the mystery of divine revelation.

To distinguish science and wisdom, metaphysics and contemplation, in order finally to unite them, has been one of the distinctive characters of the work of Jacques and Raïssa Maritain. Long ago they wrote, together, a brilliant little book on *Prayer and Intelligence*. And now, in the evening of their lives, they have given us these very pure, limpid and profoundly traditional *Notes on the Lord's Prayer*. I say "they" because almost all their works were written to some extent in collaboration, and Jacques himself has been at pains to point out his own intervention in editing these notes left him by Raïssa, for publication.

The earliest Christian treatises on "Prayer and the Spiritual Life" were not exactly what we could call, today, "works of spirituality." They were redactions of the *catechesis* or the prebaptismal instruction of catechumens. Two things above all were explained to those about to receive sacramental illumination at the sacred font, during the Vigil of Easter or Pentecost: the Creed and the Lord's Prayer. Instruction on the meaning of the Lord's Prayer, as given by the great bishops and doctors of the first Christian centuries, have therefore come down to us not simply as books of piety, or what is known in the book trade by the odious name of "inspirationals," but as simple treatises in theology: the basic theology of prayer and of the Christian life. For after all, the whole Christian life can be seen within the framework of the Our Father, which covers all man's relationships with God and with his fellow men, and brings him face to face with his most elementary and most profound responsibilities.

The Our Father is itself revelation. It is the way of prayer par excellence handed down to the Church by Christ. It is the *Oratio Dominica,* the *Lord's* Prayer, the perfect prayer, the basis of all other prayer, the source to which all other Christian prayer can be traced. We know, for example, how St. Teresa of Avila found that mystical contemplation was reducible to elements implicit in the petitions of the Our Father.

This little book of Raïssa (and Jacques) Maritain is in the pure tradition of the early catecheses on the *Pater.* Here we find not merely the voice of two learned, gifted and humble children of the Church in our time, but the clear voice of the Church herself, throughout the ages. Prayer, knowledge, worship, intelligence, devotion, and purity of life all come together and meet here in this simple yet rich theological meditation of the prayer given us by Christ in the Gospel. In this book we can find, if we seek it, the pure essence of Christian devotion.

The accents in which the book is written are, of course, contemporary. But the authors also summon to their aid the voices of the Fathers of the Church, of St. Thomas, and of modern Biblical scholars. The book becomes a confession of faith, not only of its authors, but also of the great doctors of the Church: it is another phrase in the great hymn sung by the Church to the glory of the Father.

It would therefore be a mistake to approach this book with preconceptions about contemporary fashion and controversy in the realm of prayer. It is quite true that the Maritains were identified with the Thomist positions in the dispute about contemplation that raged in the twenties. The forthcoming publication of the spiritual *Journal* kept by Raïssa will add to the annals of Christian mysticism a document of special interest and rare beauty. But this does not mean that those who are deeply engaged in the burning questions of the present moment can afford to dismiss the Maritains by putting them in a pigeonhole marked "St. John of the Cross," as if this meant that these contemplatives had no longer anything to say in an era that has rediscovered the Liturgy. Such a thought would be completely out of tune with the Second Vatican Council which, in demanding a return to the traditional

homily at Mass, is asking precisely for the kind of
instruction which we find in this book. The great
age of Liturgy was also the age of the Fathers,
and what is Liturgy itself but an elaboration of
the Last Supper and the Our Father, with read-
ings such as were familiar in the synagogue at
Christ's time? To understand the Our Father is to
get to the very root of Christian Liturgical worship.

A deceptively simple book that seems to be
purely "for beginners" is often one that is appre-
ciated most of all by those who have the most experience—for they know how true it is that everyone is always, in some sense, a beginner. Here,
then, is a book that the beginner ought to read
with interest and care: but it may well turn out to
be one that the more learned and more experienced will adopt as one of their special favorites.
Why? Precisely because it is so perfectly honest,
so unpretentious, and so simple, and because it
expounds the pure doctrine of Christ and His
Church, the riches of which are inexhaustible.

THOMAS MERTON

PREFACE

During a reunion at Kolbsheim, some ten years ago, we were discussing with a group of friends the titles of books to be included in a new collection. At that time Raïssa said at random at one point in the conversation: "Shouldn't we have a book on prayer, something like Contemplation along the Roads of the World?" Whereupon Louis Gardet declared this was just what was needed, and that Raïssa herself should write it. After that she was always thinking of this project which she could not carry out because of the trial of illness, with its interminable suffering, which constantly ravaged our little flock. But every time she could, she noted down thoughts for this Contemplation along the Roads, thoughts which came to her during prayer and certain of which made a singularly deep impress upon her mind.

13

These notes, of which she sometimes made several drafts, and which she intended to work over and complete, have, alas, fallen to me to re-copy and put into order. Those which were to comprise the first part of the book were grouped under the title *Notes on the Lord's Prayer*. I believe it is proper to publish them separately because they form a sufficient whole. I am confident that they will aid those drawn to meditation to enter more deeply into the infinite riches of the very perfect prayer taught us by Christ himself and which is the prayer above all others.

In conformity with Raïssa's expressed wish —for that matter we always submitted to each other what we wrote—I have taken it upon myself to supplement her work where it appeared necessary. Sometimes it was a question of things clearly implied in the themes she intended treating and which merely lacked sufficient development—in particular, things which she said to me on several occasions and which I remember very exactly: in such cases I simply incorporated them into the text,[1] certain that I was expressing her thought.

Sometimes it was a question of things that seemed called forth by her reflections, but which we did not discuss verbally in an explicit manner,

[1] At the same time it seemed to me useless to make a distinction between the citations figuring in her notes and those I myself added (although the first, unlike the others, played a part in the movement of her meditation).

or which were not clearly contained in her plan as I knew it: in such cases I have used a special typographical sign to denote that these additions do not engage her, although I have made them only with the thought she would have approved them.

May it be, as I hope, that at no time in the course of this work have I departed from her help and inspiration.

JACQUES MARITAIN
Fraternité, Toulouse

CONTENTS

Chapter I

THE LORD'S PRAYER

The Charity of Christ has provided us with the essential prayer—the Lord's Prayer, the prayer that is universally true and needed. *Oratio Dominica perfectissima est.*[1] In itself it is enlightenment and revelation. From the words of Christ, the Word Incarnate, we know in a very certain way, henceforth unveiled and glowing in our hearts, that we have a Father in heaven— *Pater noster qui es in coelis*—a God who loves with paternal tenderness, and not only a Creator. God takes delight in all that he has made ("God saw all the things that he had made, and they were very good"[2]), but he loves only men and angels as his children.

For the pagan sages also, in particular for

[1] Saint Thomas Aquinas, *Sum. theol.*, II–II, 83, 9.
[2] Gen. 1:31.

the Stoics, the name Father was doubtless befitting to God, but in an entirely different sense, referring only to the Principle of the cosmos as the universal First Cause: God was our Father because he had begotten us, and because his spark in us caused us to be marked with a resemblance to him. Even in the Old Testament the true meaning of divine Fatherhood remained implicit and was not unveiled. "Fatherhood was the attribute of God the Creator and the God of providence." [3] It was the Only Son, who dwells in the bosom of the Father, who "told" us of this God whom "no man hath seen at any time." [4] "All things have been delivered to me by my Father; and no one knoweth the Son except the Father, nor doth anyone know the Father except the Son, and he to whom the Son may choose to reveal him." [5] Father in an absolutely unique sense for Jesus, whose Person is consubstantial and identical in nature with the First Person of the Trinity, God is Father for his adopted sons in a sense which Jesus alone revealed: He calls us to share —through the supernatural gift of grace—in his intimate life, his possessions, his beatitude, in the heritage of his incomprehensible and infinitely transcendent Godhead, and to become "perfect even as your heavenly Father is perfect." [6]

[3] M. J. Lagrange, *Evang. selon saint Luc,* p. 321, n. 2.
[4] John 1:8.
[5] Matt. 11:27.
[6] Matt. 5:48.

"By the very name Father, we confess the remission of sins, sanctification, redemption, adoption, inheritance, our bond of brotherhood with
the only Son, and the gifts of the Spirit." [7]

*

Tertullian said that the Lord's Prayer is the
breviary of the entire Gospel.[8]

Like the Gospel, the Lord's Prayer has deep
roots in Judaism, and carries the religion of
Israel to its supreme point of perfection and
flowering, but through the descent of a higher
grace and of an absolutely transcendent element.

It has been remarked that many features of
the formulas of the Lord's Prayer resemble certain formulas of Jewish prayer and seem to be
derived from them. But in drawing upon the
treasure of his people's tradition, Jesus transfigured what he took. Despite the material resemblance, an infinite distance remains between the
Lord's Prayer and Jewish prayer. The Spirit has
renewed and superelevated everything.

Not only is the entire Lord's Prayer free
from the slightest human accrescence or super-
fluity and divinely reduced to the essential, as a
piece of gold that is miraculously purified, not

---

[7] Saint John Chrysostom, *Hom. 19,* in *Matt. 6,* n. 4., *Patrologia Graeca,* 57, 278.

[8] *De Orat.,* cap. 1, *Patrologia Latina,* 1, 1153.

only does its brevity contrast with the lengthy passages (however beautiful they may be but which the precious gems of our words make too burdensome) of the benedictions of Jewish prayer, but also and above all the universality of the spiritual kingdom and of the divine Fatherhood has eliminated from it any element of national particularism. "That exceedingly earnest and moving supplication which the Jews made on behalf of Israel is omitted. As charity ought to embrace all men, so the prayer is deemed to be uttered by all the faithful speaking as one to the one true God, who is the Father of them all." [9]

★

The Lord's Prayer is reported by Saint Luke in a slightly abbreviated form (11:2–4), and in its complete form by Saint Matthew (6:9–13). It is composed, Father Lagrange tells us, of six petitions in two series, "the first three being desires relating to God's glory; the last three being petitions in behalf of man." [10] With more reason, we

[9] M. J. Lagrange, *The Gospel of Jesus Christ*. Translated by the members of the English Dominican Province (Westminster, Md.: Newman Press, 1958), vol. II, p. 15.

[10] M. J. Lagrange, *Evang. selon saint Matthieu*, p. 126. "St. Matthew's six petitions plus an invocation form the perfect number."—M. J. Lagrange, *The Gospel of Jesus Christ, op. cit.,* vol. II, p. 15, n. 7.

believe, Saint Thomas holds to the traditional number of seven petitions [11] (*sed libera nos a malo* is then regarded as not included in the sixth petition: *et ne nos inducas in tentationem,* but as forming a distinct petition).

This prayer begins in a turning toward God and the goodness of God. In the first three petitions Christ unites us to himself in solemn and admirable supplications, Jesus' desires and our own, addressed to the common Father: Hallowed be Thy Name—Thy Kingdom come—Thy Will be done on earth as it is in heaven.

Christ permits us to join with him in addressing these mysterious supplications to our Father and his, as if our will and the sanctity, or the effort toward sanctity of his human creatures, were an aid brought to God himself in his struggle against evil, against the spirit of evil. Did not God decree for man's salvation the Incarnation of the Word into frail humanity, and the redemptive Passion of his Only Son "obedient unto death, even unto the death of the cross"? Each man is called upon to take part in this great combat led by the Son for the highest glory of the Father, because each man —in one manner or another, even the most imperfect and remote, and merely because he is born

[11] *Sum. theol.,* II–II, 83, 9.—The tradition of which we speak here has Saint Augustine as its highest authority. Origen and Saint John Chrysostom regarded the Lord's Prayer as composed of six petitions. Cf. Lagrange, *Evang. selon saint Matthieu,* p. 131, n. 12.

into the world—is a member of Christ, the head of Humanity,[12] and head of the Mystical Body which magnetizes and draws Humanity to himself.

Therefore we must pray to God for God.

꙳ It is very true that the first three petitions of the Lord's Prayer relate to a certain comportment on the part of men—such that the ineffable Name be glorified among us, that God's kingdom come about in mankind, and that his will be done by us and in us. When you ask that the Father's name be hallowed, "to look at the matter closely," wrote Saint Augustine, "thou art asking this for thyself." [13] Yes, doubtless, but for what good do you ask first and above all if it is not the glory of Him who is your absolute supreme

[12] *Sum. theol.*, III, 8, 3. "Christus est caput omnium hominum . . . Membra corporis mystici non solum accipiuntur secundum quod sunt in actu, sed etiam secundum quod sunt in potentia." ("Christ is the head of all men . . . members of the mystical body not only as they are in act, but as they are in potentiality.")

[13] Cum rogas ut sanctificetur nomen ipsius, nonne quasi pro illo illum rogas, et non pro te?" Intellige, et pro te rogas. *Serm.* 56, cap. 4, n. 5, *P.L.*, 38, 379. Cf. *ibid.*, cap. 5, n. 7, *P.L.*, 38, 380, with regard to the second petition, *fiat voluntas tua:* "Ut ergo fiat a te, non sine causa oras, nisi ut bene sit tibi."

Saint Augustine fully recognized that the first three petitions form a group different from the other four, but only in the sense, according to him, that they would be accomplished—fully—only in eternity; whereas the last four petitions concern solely our life in time. *De Serm. Domini in monte*, lib. II, cap. 10, *P.L.*, 34, 1285–1286. Let us note, however, that in *De Serm. Domini in monte* we find no trace of the idea supported in *Serm.* 56 and in the *Letter to Proba*, namely, that in the first three petitions we pray only for ourselves.

End as he is that of all created things; the accomplishment of the sovereignly good designs of Him whom you love more than yourself and above all created things; and satisfaction of the tenderness and generosity with which he loves you freely with a love that is but one with his necessary love of Himself? So that to look at it even more closely, it is for God and the Good of God that the first three petitions of the Lord's Prayer would have you pray *first and above all else.*[14] Your own good is here implied only as a secondary consideration.

Saint Augustine's great concern was to place us on guard against the idea that God could receive anything whatsoever from the creature, or that the creature's efforts could add anything to Uncreated Good. However, we should not, out of fear of a manifestly absurd idea, turn our eyes away from the sublime mystery of truth referred to in the first three petitions of the Lord's Prayer and which Saint Paul expressed by saying that we

---

[14] This is what Saint Thomas teaches regarding the first petition of the Lord's Prayer (II–II, 83, 9). We believe with Father Lagrange that it is the same for the other two petitions which are joined to it. Cf. Lagrange, *Evang. selon saint Matthieu*, p. 126, n. 8 (cited above, p. 22, n. 10). And again, *ibid*, p. 127, n. 9: "But one can also consider of primary importance the honor and in some way the good of God. The human soul can raise itself no higher than by this benevolent love, this true friendship which incites in itself desires in behalf of the sovereign good it loves." —P. 128, n. 9: "We can desire the spread of God's holiness for his own sake without thinking of the spiritual benefit we will draw from it."—P. 129, n. 10: "The three elevations descend in an admirable order from God to man, who will be more directly on the scene in the last three petitions."

are God's coadjutors, *Dei enim sumus adjutores.*[15] In the joy that God takes in his saints, in the return of the prodigal son, in the love of men and of angels—and above all in the perfect charity and obedience of Christ Jesus—there is nothing, absolutely nothing by which the creature could add anything whatsoever to the superexcellent fullness of the divine Being. On the contrary, as it is God who causes the creature, and the liberty of the latter moved by Him, to participate in the work which He himself accomplishes in accordance with the eternal designs, so also it is God who in virtue of the superabundance of his charity causes the loving responses of his creatures, the offerings and the gifts to which his Grace induces them, to enter into the very joy and exultation of love which are identical with his immutable essence and through which he delights eternally in himself.[16] The manifestation *ad extra* of his glory adds nothing to this glory which is his by necessity of nature, but he has freely willed from all eternity that while unfurling itself in time it be fully possessed on high by the eternal glory in which it shares, and receive from it all its effulgence. ☞

We see in what sense it is right to say that we should pray to God for God. We should first and before all desire, seek, and pursue the good of this

---

[15] 1 Cor. 3:9.

[16] Cf. John of Saint Thomas, *Cursus theol.,* t. III, disp. 4 a. 4 and 5 (on the liberty of the divine will, and of its immanent acts in regard to creatures).

God whom we dearly love, and ask him that the manifestation of his glory and of his goodness be finally accomplished. Through the merits of Christ's Passion—uniting ourselves with it and living in divine grace and charity—we should first and before all else aspire in heart and action that we ourselves and every immortal soul should bear witness to the holiness of the heavenly Father and render his Name blessed on earth; that we should hasten the expansion of his Reign and the final coming of his Kingdom, triumphant over every other power; that we should accomplish here below his adorable Will, so that through love it may finally be established also on earth as it is established in heaven.

We should pray that charity may in the end transfigure this world and invest it with a divine character, finally liberating it from the kinds of rights, if one may so speak, which the Prince of this world has exercised over it.

★

And that charity may reign in us, we should pray for ourselves in the manner taught us by Jesus in the continuation of the Lord's Prayer.

Panem nostrum quotidianum da nobis hodie. Here begins the prayer of sinners for themselves. We ask daily bread for our bodies and for our souls; pardon for our sins, in return for the mercy we show toward those who have offended us; we ask our heavenly Father to guard us from the dangers of temptation and for him to deliver us from evil.

He will do this because He loves us and because He is the source of all good. And without this what could we offer him? The gifts that children make wholeheartedly to their father are always drawn in some measure from that father's wealth.

Chapter II

THE FIRST THREE PETITIONS

1

OUR FATHER

Jesus Christ taught us to say *Our Father,* and not *My Father.*

~ This is because, as Saint Thomas Aquinas writes,[1] "God's love is not restricted to any individual, but embraces all in common; for God loves all things that are. . . . Most of all he loves men. . . . At the same time we should

---

[1] Saint Thomas Aquinas, *Compendium Theologiae,* II, cap. 5; in *Opuscula Theologica* (Turin: Marietti, 1954), t. I, n. 557 and 558. English trans. by Cyril Vollert, S.J., *Compendium of Theology* by Saint Thomas Aquinas (St. Louis and London: B. Herder Book Co., 1958), pp. 319–20.

remember that, although our hope rests chiefly on God's help, we can aid one another to obtain more easily what we ask for. . . . As Ambrose reminds us [2]: 'Many insignificant people, when they are gathered together and are of one mind, become powerful, and the prayers of many cannot but be heard.' This agrees with Matthew 18:19: 'If two of you shall consent on earth concerning anything whatsoever for which they shall ask, it shall be done to them by my Father who is in heaven.' Therefore we do not pour forth our prayers as individuals, but with unanimous accord we cry out 'Our Father,' even when one each of us prays *clauso ostio*.

"Let us also reflect that our hope reaches up to God through Christ, according to Romans 5:1–2. . . . Through him who is the only-begotten Son of God by nature, we are made adopted sons . . . as is said in Galatians 4:4–5. Hence, in acknowledging that God is our Father, we should do so in such a way as not to disparage the prerogative of the Only-begotten," who alone has the special right to say, *My Father.*

WHO ART IN HEAVEN

"Wherefore should the nations say: 'Where then is their God?'

[2] More precisely, as attributed to Saint Ambrose (Ambrosiaster, *in Rom.,* cap. 15, *P.L.,* 17, 186–7).

"Nay, our God is in the heavens. He doth whatsoever pleaseth him." [3]

Speaking of the Patriarchs, they acknowledged, says Saint Paul,[4] that they were " 'strangers and sojourners on earth.' For those who say such things make it plain that they search for a fatherland. . . .

"As it is, they long for a *better fatherland, that is, a heavenly one.* Whence God is not ashamed to be called their God, for he hath prepared for them a city. . . ."

And again [5]: "For us, *our country is in the heavens;*

"whence we eagerly await as saviour the Lord Jesus Christ;

"who will transform the body of our lowliness [the body of the *"earthly man"* [6]]

"that it may be one with the body of his glory [the body of the *"celestial man"* [7]]

"by the force of that power whereby he is able to subject all things to himself."

What are, then, those heavens in which our Father lives, and where our city is found, and which is the fatherland to which we aspire, and where our "life is hidden with Christ in God"? [8]

[3] Ps. 113:10 (Vulgate Ps. 113, pt. 2:2).
[4] Heb. 11:13–16.
[5] Philipp. 3:20–21.
[6] 1 Cor. 15:47.
[7] *Ibid.*, 15:48–49.
[8] Col. 3:3.

This is a mystery that infinitely surpasses every idea the human mind can attempt to express in halting words. It is an astonishing thing that the Beyond which is more important for us than everything here below, on which our hope hangs, and which God "has prepared for those he loves," draws us all the more powerfully the thicker the veil that covers it—"what eye hath not seen, what ear hath not heard, what hath not entered into heart of man . . ." [9]

Nevertheless faith, in its obscure manner, teaches us something of it. Heaven, or the heavens, is doubtless, as is sometimes said,[10] souls in the state of grace wherein the Trinity dwells, and in particular the souls of the saints.[11]

∿ "There is an obstacle to prayer or confidence in God," Saint Thomas remarks,[12] "that would deter one from praying. This is the notion that human life is far removed from divine providence. The thought is given expression, in the person of the wicked, in Job 22:14: 'The clouds are his covert, and he doth not consider our things, and he walketh about the poles of heaven'; also in

[9] Saint Paul, 1 Cor. 2:9. (Cf. Isaias 64:3, and Jeremias 3:16).

[10] M. J. Lagrange, *The Gospel of Jesus Christ, op. cit.*, II, p. 212.

[11] Cf. Saint Cyril of Jerusalem, *Catéchèses mystag.*, IX, *P.G.*, 33, 1177: "The heavens also mean those who bear in them the image of the celestial man, in whom God dwells and walks"; and Saint Augustine, *De Serm. Dom. in monte*, lib. II, cap. 5: ". . . In coelis, id est, in sanctis et justis." *P.L.*, 34, 1276.

[12] *Compendium Theologiae*, II, cap. 6 (Marietti), t. 1, n. 562 to 564. English trans. by Vollert, *op. cit*, pp. 322–3.

Ezechiel 8:12: 'The Lord seeth us not, the Lord hath forsaken the earth.'

"But the Apostle Paul taught the contrary in his sermon to the Athenians, when he said that God is 'not far from every one of us; for in him we live and move and are' (Acts 17:27–8). . . . We are told in Matthew 10:29–31: 'Are not two sparrows sold for a farthing? And not one of them shall fall to the ground without your Father. But the very hairs of your head are all numbered' . . . thus indicating that everything belonging to man is to be recovered at the resurrection . . . As our Lord adds, in the same context: 'Fear not, therefore; better are you than many sparrows' (Matt. 10:31). This clarifies the passage: 'The children of men shall put their trust under the covert of thy wings' (Ps. 36 [35]:8).

"Although God is said to be near all men by reason of his special care over them, he is exceptionally close to the good who strive to draw near to him in faith and love. . . . Indeed, he not only draws nigh to them: he even dwells in them through grace. . . . Therefore, to increase the hope of the saints, we are bidden to say: 'who art in heaven,' that is, in the saints, as Augustine explains. For, as the same doctor adds, the spiritual distance between the just and sinners seems to be as great as the spatial distance between heaven and earth. . . . He who has made them heavens will not withhold heavenly goods from them." ✒

Nevertheless heaven, or the heavens, or the "things that are above," [13] is also and first of all —is essentially—the other world where God is loved and obeyed in an absolutely perfect manner by the blessed and by the angels,[14] where the sons of God are revealed,[15] and where creation enters into the freedom of the glory of the sons of God [16]; "heaven is where sin has ceased, heaven is where the wound of death exists no more [17]; it is the "light inaccessible" where dwells the Blessed and only Sovereign" [18]; it is the universe of the beatific vision, the Church triumphant and the Jerusalem on high, which has existed from the beginning with the holy Angels steadfast in their allegiance to God, and which will attain its fullness with the resurrected and thenceforth "spiritual" bodies of the just, formed to "the likeness of the heavenly man," [19] when Christ will have "put . . . under his feet," "the last enemy," which is "death." Then "he will say: 'he hath subjected all things.'" [20]

This is the world where, because it is a divinified world, the Father dwells—as he dwells already in the souls of the saints here below, but there in a still higher manner—altogether *at home*

---

[13] Saint Paul, Col. 3:1–2.
[14] Cf. Saint Augustine, *Ep. ad Probam, P.L.,* 33, 502 (n. 21); and *De Serm. Domini in monte,* lib. II, cap. 6, *P.L.,* 34, 1278.
[15] Saint Paul, Rom. 8:19.
[16] *Ibid.,* 8:21.
[17] Saint Ambrose, *De Sacram.,* lib. VI, n. 20, *P.L.,* 16, 451.
[18] Saint Paul, 1 Tim. 6, 15–16.
[19] Saint Paul, 1 Cor. 15:44,49.
[20] *Ibid.,* 15:26–27.

and content, finding there no obstacle at all to his love. It is a world of whose existence we know from revelation, but whose nature and laws are impenetrable to us. It is a heaven whose azure is a veil beyond which our gaze does not pass. At night it gleams with stars, but we have no telescopes to bring these stars of the night of faith closer to us.

Lord Jesus, have pity on us therefore and on our poor world. Grant that we may conquer through love the power over this world which You accorded to Lucifer from the moment of his creation, and which remains despite his sin, and to which our sins enslave us.

This love is the very life of Your grace, which we have to receive and to keep faithfully.

Our power lies in fidelity to Your grace.

Lucifer's power lies in his creaturely princedom over the things of the world.

Jesus' power lies in His supreme fidelity— He, God incarnate in our miserable body—the Incarnate Word Jesus who won for his Humanity "the power to subject all things to himself."

HALLOWED BE THY NAME

"He who would offer a worthy prayer to God," says Saint Thomas,[21] quoting Saint John

---

[21] *Compendium Theologiae,* II, cap. 8 (Marietti), t. I, n. 572; English trans. Vollert, *op. cit.,* p. 329.—Saint John Chrysostom, *Hom. 19,* in *Matt.* 6, n. 4, *P.G.,* 57, 279.

Chrysostom, "should ask for nothing before the Father's glory, but should make everything come after the praise of him."

Hallowed be Thy name. "By whom would God be sanctified, since it is he who sanctifies?" [22] But He said: "Be holy because I am holy." [23] It is by sanctifying ourselves that we glorify our Father's Name.[24] Thus we can repair the injustice done to him by this misguided world: "My name is continually blasphemed all the day long." [25] Jesus himself rendered perfect glory to this Name.

"I have glorified thee upon earth. . . .

"I have manifested thy name to the men whom thou hast given me out of the world. . . .

"Just Father,

indeed the world hath not known thee,

but I have known thee,

and these have known

that thou sent me;

and I have made known thy name to them,

and will make it known,

in order that the love wherewith thou hast loved me

---

[22] Saint Cyprian, *De Orat. Domin.*, n. 12, *P.L.*, 4, 527.

[23] Levit. 11:44.

[24] As Father Lagrange very rightly points out, God's inaccessible holiness demands to be communicated. To pray for the hallowing of his Name is to pray for the full accomplishment of the work of holiness which is his, and in which those who live in his grace will be associated throughout all time (Cf. Lagrange, *Evang. selon saint Matthieu*, p. 128, n. 9).

[25] Isaias 52:5.

may be in them
and I in them." [26]

And to us Jesus has given this precept: "Let your light shine before men, in order that they may see your good works and glorify your Father who is in the heavens." [27]

Thus we should ask that the Father's Name be hallowed in us; and not only in us, as Tertullian remarks,[28] but in all men, especially in those whom the grace of God still awaits, and in those whom we hold to be our enemies, since we are also required to pray for them.

Hallowed be *Thy Name*.

➤ We know that in the Semitic languages the word *name* has so much force that in signifying the named it reveals in some way its essence. With the progress of time the word has lost little by little the magic power with which it was invested primitively, and in virtue of which the knowledge of the Name gave power over the Named.[29] The name which "both designates and

[26] John 17:4, 6, 25–26.

[27] Matt. 5:16.

[28] Cf. *De Oratione,* cap. 4, *P.L.,* I, 1157.

[29] "The uttering of the Name gives as it were a power over the Named, the 'seal of the name' being in a way an entrance into communication with the intimate nature of the Named." Louis Gardet, *Mystique musulmane* (Paris: Vrin, 1961), p. 199. This remark also applies to Jewish thought; and even, as the author indicates, to Buddhist thought, and in a certain measure to the thought of the Christian East ("The Prayer of Jesus").

veils the named," [30] nevertheless retained for the
Jews of the Hellenistic era a value so intensely and
even so exaggeratedly realistic that to know and
utter someone's name was to manifest this someone himself as it were by seizing him under a veil.
Thy Name is Thyself, Thyself as designated in
Thy hidden secret. ✒

To speak truly, however, it is only in God
that there is identity between Name and Named.
Far rather than the Names we use to designate
God, the Name of which it is a question in the first
petition of the Lord's Prayer, is the ineffable Name
itself, the subsisting Name which God alone can
pronounce and which is identified with God himself. "When Jacob asked the Angel early in the
morning: 'Tell me, what is your name?' he replied,
'Why do you ask my name?' It is impossible to
utter this truly wondrous name, the name that is
set above every name that is named either in the
present world or in the world to come." [31]

[30] Louis Gardet, "Al-Asma" in *L'Encyclopédie de l'Islam*
(2d ed.).

[31] Gen. 32:29; Judges 13:17–18. Cf. Saint Thomas Aquinas,
in *Librum B. Dionysii De divin. Nomin. Expositio,* cap. 1, lect. 3,
Marietti, 1950, n. 96 (free translation borrowed from *The Degrees of Knowledge,* New York, Charles Scribner's Sons, 1959,
p. 1).—Cf. *Contra Gent.,* I, cap. 31: "If we could know the divine
essence as it is in itself, and give it a name befitting to it, we would
express it by a single name. Such was the promise made by the
prophet (Zach. 14:9, to whose text Saint Thomas here gives its
highest eschatological meaning) to those who will see him in his
essence: 'In that day there shall be one Yahweh and his name
shall be one.' "

"It will not be," Monsignor Journet admirably comments, "a

Mystery of divine Revelation! This Name set above every other name can itself be designated—but at a distance, the distance that separates the Infinite from the finite [32]—by a name which our lips can utter. Thus it is that the ineffable Name was first revealed to Moses, and mysteriously symbolized by the tetragrammaton. At a certain moment in their history the Jews—through a feeling of reverent fear and holy trembling in which the logic of their way of semi-identifying the name with the named was pushed to its extreme limit—had to decide no longer to pronounce it at all.[33] The word *Adonai* (my Lord) henceforth replaced that of *Yahweh*.

---

sonorous name that can be pronounced in one of the human languages. It will be a name of fire and of light, a spiritual name, pervasive and subsisting. It will be uttered in the hearts of the elect and of the angels immerged in Him as is the sponge in the ocean, by the divine essence itself, capable *in itself* of denoting all its transparency and plenitude. Nevertheless, *in fact,* no creature will ever possess it to the point of exhausting its content or of circumscribing its riches: for it is absolutely necessary to be all that God is in order to know absolutely what God is." Charles Journet, *Connaissance et Inconnaissance de Dieu* (Fribourg and Paris: Ed. Egloff, 1943), p. 58.

[32] It is a question here of our knowledge of God. If, on the other hand, it is a question of God's knowledge of us and of the care with which his providence watches over us, we must say, as we have seen above (p. 33), that God is not far from us, that he is very close to men.

[33] "It was not in the first place," Father Lagrange writes, "because the Jews feared that the Gentiles were making magic use of the sacred name that they forbade its use among themselves: it was rather because the Jews regarded this name as a formidable mystery that the pagans liked to use it in their magic rites. In ancient times, it was the common patrimony of the Israelites; it was not forbidden them. On the contrary, they pronounced it with

But the ineffable Name was not only revealed to Moses from the midst of the burning
bush and the fiery flame, and in a sign—"I Am
Who Am," or "I Am Who I Am (and Whom I
alone know)"—which was to become unpro-
nounceable and undecipherable for the people of
God.

It has also been revealed to all of us by Jesus,
on the roadways and humble hills where he and
his disciples did their preaching—and in the word
which is the most easily pronounced by the poorest
children of men.

For by this time it is no longer a question of a
name which one would wish, attempting the impossible, to render in our human signs as incom-
municable as the very Name of God in God (as if
the "I AM" of Horeb,[34] as well as all the other
names by which God makes himself known to us,
were not a sign among others which the mirror of
creatures offers our minds).

This time it is a question of a very simple
name in our language, which declares from the
very first (as befits a revelation that is not reserved
to any one people alone, but cast to all the ends of

---

love in their pious outpourings. The reserve of Hellenistic times
implies that many Israelites had become too worldly to use it"
(M. J. Lagrange, *Le Judaisme avant Jésus-Christ*, Paris, 1931,
p. 459). It could also be said, and more correctly in our opinion,
that this reserve sprang from a more and more explicitly felt
communication, to the Name revealed to us, of the sacred terror
inspired by the transcendence of the Named.

[34] Exod. 3:14.

the earth) that the reflection of the beyond in the
mirror of creatures [35] is the sole means by which
God can be known and make himself known to
us. He is the Father of us all, and the Father from
whom proceeds the uncreated Word, incarnate in
Jesus. "If ye love me, ye will keep my commandments. And *I will ask the Father,* and he shall
give you another Advocate, that he may be with
you forever." [36] . . . "If any one loveth me, he
will keep my word, and *my Father* shall love him,
and *we* will come to him." [37] . . . Whatsoever
you ask *the Father in my name,* he will give it
you." [38] . . . "As thou, Father, art in me, and I
in thee, that they too may be in us." [39]

Thus in one breath we say: God One and
Triune, who made heaven and earth, You our
Father who are in heaven; Father of the only Son
and of us who are his brethren by adoption, You
our Father who are in heaven.

And by this very Name of Father we are
taught that he is Love, Mercy, and Goodness.

Nevertheless, do not believe, my poor
soul, that with this name of Father, or of Love and
of Goodness, the distance between Him and thee

[35] Let us say, to employ the vocabulary of the philosophers,
the analogy of anoetic rational knowledge or the superanalogy
of faith. (Cf. J. Maritain, *The Degrees of Knowledge, op. cit.,*
pp. 222–6, 241–4.)

[36] John 14:15–16.

[37] *Ibid.,* 14:23.

[38] *Ibid.,* 15:16.

[39] *Ibid.,* 17:21.

is any less great [40] than it is with the name we are
forbidden to spell out. For He eludes every grasp
and His transcendence makes Him all the more
unknown the more thou knowest Him. He is—in
an infinitely better way than anything else is, but
also and by that very fact in a way altogether
different from the way which anything else is. He
is Father—in an infinitely better way than any of
us is father, but also and by that very fact in a way
altogether different from the way in which any of
us is a father. He loves thee—in an infinitely better
way than any creature can love, but also and by
that very fact He loves thee in an altogether different manner, a manner that thou art absolutely
incapable of imagining.

And when the great trial comes to thee, this
altogether different of His Fatherhood and of His
love will nail thee to the Cross,

> *O divine Cross, bitter wood,*
> *Bloody price of the Beatitudes,*[41]

the more cruelly still than the *altogether different*
of his being. ✍

★

In meditating on all these things, we see that
if we were to try to express in other words the

[40] Cf. above, p. 39, n. 32.
[41] Raïssa Maritain, "O Croix," in *Au Creux du Rocher* (Paris: Alsatia, n.d.).

meaning of the first petition of the Lord's Prayer, we should have to say:

O God, One and Triune, who art our Father, O First Person of the Trinity who art the Father of the Only Son and of us who are your adopted sons,

May glory be rendered Thy ineffable holiness; may Thy name, which is Thyself, be manifested, praised and blessed in us and in every creature. *Ita fac nos vivere, ut per nos te universi glorificent* [42]—grant us to live in such a way that through us all that there is in the world may glorify Thee.

[42] Saint John Chrysostom, *Hom. 19, in Matt.*, 6, n. 4, *P.G.*, 57, 279, cited by Saint Thomas, *Compendium Theologiae*, II, cap. 8 (Marietti), n. 572; Eng. trans., *op. cit.*, p. 325.

2

THY KINGDOM COME

☙ *Adveniat regnum tuum,* Ἐλθέτω ἡ βασιλεία σου. The Greek word *basileia,* the Latin word *regnum,* signify both *reign* and *kingdom.* These two meanings do not exclude each other; on the contrary, they evoke each other. Nevertheless we may ask which of the two, in the second petition of the Lord's Prayer, has the primary importance.

To this Father Lagrange replies [1] that there can be no question of saying, "Thy Kingdom come," because a kingdom does not come—a manifestly feeble reason, because it is entirely normal to speak of the *advent* of a kingdom; and a kingdom *comes* when it is established and when it extends itself, and if a reign "comes," it is, be it more or less implicitly, together with a kingdom over which it rules and which itself conjointly "comes" or "arrives."

Indeed, if *Reign* is ordinarily used in French

[1] *Evang. selon saint Luc,* p. 322, n. 2.

44

translations of the Lord's Prayer, *Kingdom* is
ordinarily used in the English and German translations (*Kingdom, Reich*), and it is particularly
noteworthy that in translations into Semitic languages a word meaning first of all *Kingdom* is
used. This is the case in the current Hebrew translation (*Malkout,* a modern translation, it is true),
and, in a still more significant way, in the Arabic
translation offered by the Greek-Catholic rite; not
only is it a question here of a translation conse-
crated by liturgical usage and by time, but in recit-
ing the Lord's Prayer at Mass one says *Malakout,*
which signifies *Kingdom,* whereas at the beginning
of the Mass in speaking of God's reign one uses
another word (*Mamlakat*) which explicitly signifies *Reign* and not *Kingdom.*

Without thereby excluding the meaning of
"reign," we shall thus prefer to say: "Thy Kingdom come." And at the same time we shall understand that in the Lord's Prayer Jesus did not teach
us to ask only in a general way for God to be
obeyed by all, but also to ask in a more precise and
explicit manner for the coming of that Kingdom
of God or Kingdom of heaven [2] which he came to

[2] "From the first days of his public life, Jesus proclaims:
'the kingdom of the heavens is at hand' (Matt. 4:17). . . . All
throughout his mission 'the kingdom of the heavens' came constantly to his lips. The expression is typically Palestinian (Mark
and Luke translate it according to Greco-Roman usage: 'the kingdom of God.')." Augustin George, S.M., *Connaître Jésus-Christ*
(Paris: Equipes Enseignantes, 18 rue Ernest-Lacoste, 1960), p.
41.

proclaim,[3] and concerning which his thought and his preaching abounded in inexhaustible parables which the Gospels constantly present to us.

But what is this Kingdom if it is not the Church which is in this world but not of this world—*regnum meum non est de hoc mundo* [4]— the Church considered not as it existed before Christ, under inchoate and masked forms, but as together with Christ, especially after Pentecost, it will appear among us with face uncovered and in the resplendent vigor of its Head, the Incarnate Word? And it is also the Church of the hereafter, not according as before Christ it gathered the elect together in the bosom of Abraham, but as it will rejoice in vision once Christ enters into his glory, and as it will finally attain to its complete fullness with the resurrection of the body.

"Until John, there were the Law and the prophets; thenceforth the Gospel of God's kingdom and everyone [of those who have ears to hear] is forcing his way into it" [5]—"the violent [those who do not hesitate to cut off their right hand if it gives them scandal and to love Jesus more than father or mother] have been seizing it by force." [6] "Amen, I say to you, among those born of woman there has not risen greater than John

[3] *Oportet me evangelizare regnum Dei.* Luke 4:43.
[4] John 18:36.
[5] Luke 16:16.
[6] Matt. 11:12.

the Baptist; yet the least in the kingdom of heaven [according as he has the grace of Christ already come and he is called no longer to wait in limbo but to see God face to face in heaven] is greater than he." [7] ✍

★

Thy Kingdom come. This petition, or this desire, relates first and above all to the future world, the world of eternity where alone the first petition also, "Hallowed be Thy Name," will be accomplished in an absolutely perfect manner. "It is quite evident that the petition concerns the future." [8] "The Kingdom of God, for whose coming we ask, has its term in the consummation of the world." [9] "The kingdom of God within us, who are tireless marchers, will reach its perfection when the words of the Apostle [10] are accomplished: 'When He shall have put all his enemies under his feet, He shall deliver up the Kingdom to his Father, in order that God may be all in all.'" [11] "What then is this kingdom you desire to come? It is the one spoken of in the Gospel [12]: 'Come, ye blessed of my Father, inherit the kingdom pre-

[7] *Ibid.,* 11:11.
[8] M. J. Lagrange, *Evang. selon saint Luc,* p. 322 n.
[9] Tertullian, *De Oratione,* cap. 5, *P.L.,* I, 1159.
[10] 1 Cor. 15:24–28 (condensed).
[11] Origen, *De Oratione,* 25, *P.G.,* 11, 497.
[12] Matt. 25:34.

pared for you from the foundation of the world.' " [13] This Kingdom is the Church triumphant. "Then shall the just shine forth as the sun in the kingdom of the Father." [14]

And what did the Old Testament say earlier? Wisdom "showed him [the just] the kingdom of God," [15] when Jacob in his dream saw the ladder standing upon the earth and the top thereof reaching heaven, and the angels of God ascending and descending.[16] "The God of heaven will set up a kingdom that shall never be destroyed, . . . and itself shall stand for ever." [17] "His kingdom is an everlasting kingdom." [18] *"Et regnum ejus in generationem et generationem."* [19] "One like the Son of man came with the clouds of heaven. . . . His power is an everlasting power . . . and his kingdom shall not be destroyed." [20] "The saints of the most high God shall take the kingdom: and they shall possess the kingdom for ever and ever." [21]

"Saviours shall come up into mount Sion to judge the mount of Esau: and the kingdom shall be for the Lord." [22]

[13] Saint Augustine, *Serm.* 56, cap. 4, n. 6., *P.L.* 38, 379.
[14] Matt. 13:43.
[15] Wis. 10:10.
[16] Gen. 28:12.—"In thee and thy seed all the tribes of the earth shall be blessed."
[17] Daniel 2:44.
[18] *Ibid.,* 3:100 (and 4:31).
[19] *Ibid.,* 4:31.
[20] *Ibid.,* 7:13–14.
[21] *Ibid.,* 7:18 (Cf. 7:27).
[22] Abdias, 21.

But the second petition of the Lord's Prayer refers also to a kingdom already present, which has to expand and win more and more the depth of the human being and of human life. "The kingdom of God has come when you have received his grace. Indeed he himself said [23]: 'The kingdom of God is within you.' " [24]

Interrogatus autem a Pharisaeis: quando venit regnum Dei? respondens eis dixit: Non venit regnum Dei cum observatione. Neque dicent: Ecce hic, aut ecce illic. Ecce enim regnum Dei intra vos est. [25] Let us try to disengage the meaning of these lines of Saint Luke, quoted by Saint Ambrose in the passage just mentioned: "On being asked by the Pharisees when the kingdom of God would come, he answered them and said: The kingdom of God cometh unawares"— it cannot be awaited like a material event, as the coming of an army in clouds of dust and with arms glittering in the sun—"as if one could say: 'Behold, it is here,' or, 'it is there.' For behold, the Kingdom of the grace of Christ come among men is within you," or, according to an equally authoritative translation, "among you." [26] "It is already among you: you have not seen it because it does

[23] Luke 17:21.
[24] Saint Ambrose, *De Sacram.*, lib. VI, n. 22, *P.L.*, 16, 451.
[25] Luke 17:20–21.
[26] We have used both Father Lagrange's translation [also corresponding to that of most English translations of the Bible] which says "within you," and that of the Jerusalem Bible which says "among you."

not come as a finished thing of which it can be said that it is here or it is there, but by looking at it closely we can recognize it as a seed which is growing." [27]

It is among you, or within you, as the Kingdom of Christ's grace come among men—it is the Church here below, the Kingdom of God "in the state of pilgrimage and crucifixion," [28] and which while visible, and composed of the just who make its visibility more resplendent and of sinners who becloud it, has as its soul and life grace and charity, and, on these grounds, is without stain or blemish, but in the depths of hearts, at that secret point where each man chooses either to allow the life of the Mystical Body to operate in him, as in a holy and active member, or chooses to evade that life as a member in whom blood no longer circulates. This is the Kingdom of God making its way on earth, in which Jesus Christ "is in agony until the end of the world" and which, step by step, by the application of the merits of Christ to each member of time, "makes up" in the course of centuries, by virtue of its union with the love and passion of its Head, for "what is lacking to the sufferings of Christ." [29]

In saying, "Thy Reign come," or "Thy Kingdom come," it is for this progressive accomplish-

[27] M. J. Lagrange, *Evang. selon saint Luc,* p. 460 n.
[28] Charles Journet, *L'Eglise du Verbe Incarné,* t. II, p. 87.
[29] Saint Paul, Col. 1:24.

ment of the work of coredemption that we are asking. We beseech God to make us advance toward the final term as "tireless marchers," and to have us cooperate in the expansion of his Kingdom, so that the Church, enlarging its boundaries without cease, may extend itself more and more among the peoples of the world and reintegrate into itself the people of Israel; that there may increase more and more the number of the saved (whether they form part of the Church's visible membership, or whether they belong to it invisibly); and that by successive stages a progress in depth may render those who in the supernatural order are "fellow citizens of the saints," more and more docile to the spirit and to the exigencies of the Gospel and more and more in accord with the charity of Jesus.

*

And we ask secondarily that in the temporal order itself and in all that which relates to its domain, the struggle which is pursued from age to age against the servitude, misery and suffering of men, the effort toward justice, civic friendship, respect for the dignity of the person, constantly win ground.

And doubtless to expect for this earth, as if it had to come about in history, the kingdom of

God fully consummated, is an absurdity, because as long as history will endure a progress in the direction of evil will coexist with a progress in the direction of good, and will thwart it. But the fact remains that the kingdom of God fully consummated will come about beyond history, with the new earth and the new heavens, when the sorting out will be made between the mass of iniquity which draws the world in the direction of its prince, and which will detach itself so as to go toward its own place, and the energies of love and of truth which draw it in the direction of its Saviour and which will detach themselves so as to go toward their own place, so that by such a rupture and blazing discontinuity the world transfigured will be absorbed into the Church triumphant, into the Kingdom of heaven which Christ will restore to his Father.

It remains that throughout the course of history, so long as there will be immortal souls bent beneath inhuman conditions of life, there cannot be on earth any rest for the Christian; it remains that, by a corollary of his supernatural vocation, the temporal mission of the Christian engages him to work in one manner or another for the common good of humanity on earth, and for the mainte- nance of man's temporal hope in the Gospel. It re- mains that for as much as the transformations of the world will take place in a manner truly bene- ficial to man and truly liberating, they will be, on the one hand, as it were a refraction, in the temporal world, of the virtues and graces of the Kingdom of God in pilgrimage here below, and, on the other, as a distant prefiguration, in the enigmas and nights of our carnal conditions, of the Kingdom of God in the glory of the world to come.

It is for this reason that these transformations indirectly concern the Kingdom of God; we ask for them indirectly in asking for the coming of this Kingdom. Why indirectly? Because they are sought first for men (although referred, of course, as is every good petition, to the glory of God as ultimate end).

*

But all that we ask directly in asking for the coming of the Kingdom of heaven, all the things which directly concern that Kingdom, and which we have previously considered—it is clear that we ask for all of this first for God, our Father and our Friend by the grace of charity, before asking it for ourselves.

We must therefore renounce following here, however great and respected they may be, those who think that the second petition of the Lord's Prayer is addressed to God for ourselves, not for God. Doubtless, as we have already remarked, and since obviously creatures are needed if God wishes that in causing them to enter freely into His joy He may consummate freely, by their means, the glory which He has necessarily and eternally by nature and to which nothing can be added, the first three petitions relate to the comportment and to the destiny of men. And this, we believe, is all that Tertullian wished to say ("We ask to reign more promptly, and to escape more quickly from bondage" [30]) or Saint Cyprian ("We pray for the coming of the promised Kingdom, purchased for us by the blood and passion of Christ. Then we who were formerly slaves in the world may reign under the sovereignty of Christ" [31]).

But Saint Augustine, fearing lest one would imagine that God does not yet reign over the things he has made, and that he will owe to our own good solicitude his reigning over them some day, assures us that in asking that his Kingdom come we are but "exciting our desire towards that reign of God *in order that it may come to us, and that we may reign in it.*" [32] And because he follows Saint Augustine, Saint Thomas Aquinas, in that invaluable masterpiece that is the *Compendium Theologiae,* restricts his commentary on the second petition of the Lord's Prayer to a long explanation of what will be our beatitude or sub-

[30] Tertullian, *De Oratione,* cap. 5, *P.L.,* I, 1159.
[31] Saint Cyprian, *De Oratione Dominica,* n. 13, *P.L.,* 4, 527.
[32] *Ad Probam, P.L.,* 33, 502 (n. 21).

jective ultimate end, and the vision by which we will enjoy God.[33] 🖝 ·

In truth, the second petition, like the first and the third, relates to the destiny and to the comportment of men. But like the other two, it is toward the good of God, not of men, that it first and above all excites our desire; it is for God that it has us pray. "An uplifting of the heart toward our Father," Father Lagrange very correctly writes, "three desires uttered by a soul united to that Father by the bonds of friendship and animated by a desire for His good: the soul's good being is the outpouring of the Father's good and returns to Him again in glory. . . ." [34]

The Lord has willed, because he loves us, that we enter into his joy [35]; the Father has willed that the Kingdom of heaven be given to his saints.[36]

And we, we will, because we love Him, that his Kingdom should increase here below, in order that there may unfold in time the work for which he sent his Son and in which his love delights; we will, because we love him, that his Kingdom, the

---

[33] *Comp. Theologiae*, II, cap. 9, Marietti, n. 573 ff. (The work, interrupted by the death of the saint, stops with the second petition.)

[34] M. J. Lagrange, *The Gospel of Jesus Christ*, vol. II, p. 16.

[35] *Intra in gaudium Domini tui*. Matt. 25:21 and 23. *Ego dispono vobis, sicut disposuit mihi Pater meus, regnum, ut edatis et bibatis super mensam meam in regno meo.* Luke 22:29–30.

[36] *Nolite timere, pusillus grex, quia complacuit Patri vestro dare vobis regnum.* Luke 12:32 (Cf. Daniel 7:18).

Kingdom which before being given to us is first of
all and will ever remain essentially his, be consummated in heaven, in order that in accordance
with his desire he may there be all and all, and
that his own praise and his own joy, as necessary
and immutable in him as his essence, may have—
through the free gift which he has made of himself to his elect, and which has been freely received by them under the motion of grace—their
eternal plenitude.

3

THY WILL BE DONE
ON EARTH AS IT IS IN HEAVEN

~ God is so lofty—and so infinite is the
fullness of his being—that in order to know, in
our human way, what in him is perfectly one and
indivisible, we need to employ a plurality of concepts. It is thus that the theologians distinguish in
the divine will several kinds of will, which they
designate by words that do not denote a particularly happy effort of verbal imagination but
which concern things very important to consider.

Let us turn first to what the theologians call
voluntas signi: this is the divine will taken (in
opposition to the *voluntas beneplaciti,* or will
properly so called) in a metaphorical sense, according as one calls "the will of God" this or that
mode of manifestation (for example, precept, pro-
hibition, counsel [1]) which for us is the sign of an

---

[1] There are five signs that manifest the divine will: prohibi-
tion, precept, counsel, operation, and permission. Cf. *Sum. theol.,*
I, 19, 12.

act of will. Those who accomplish the precepts of the Lord do his will. Therefore in saying, "Thy Will be done," we are asking that we ourselves and our brethren carry out all that the Father prescribes, avoid all that he forbids, and faithfully follow the inspiration of his counsels. ✍

This is quite evident. "If ye love me, ye will keep my commandments." [2]

★

It is well for us to meditate more at length on another theological distinction which introduces us more deeply into the impenetrable mystery. In considering the will of God properly so called, the theologians distinguish the "antecedent will"—let us say the primordial or 'uncircumstanced' will—and the "consequent will," which we may call the definitive or 'circumstanced' will. It is the definitive or circumstanced will which is always accomplished,[3] and which nothing in the world can escape; it is the *absolute* will of God. But the primordial or uncircumstanced will, that by which "God wishes all men to be saved and to come to knowledge of truth," [4] is nevertheless very real and fundamentally real, although condi-

---

[2] John 14:21.
[3] *Sum. theol.*, I, 19, 6.
[4] Saint Paul, 1 Tim. 2:4.

tional; it is not a simple velleity,[5] it is the first root
of the whole divine economy. In calling it primordial or antecedent, one clearly does not mean to
say that it precedes in time the definitive will (the
two are in God the same unique and sublime
eternal will; priority and posteriority are only of
the logical order and concern only our human
mode of thinking); in calling it primordial or antecedent we wish to say that as concerns the logical order of increasing determination under which
the object willed is taken, it is that original im-
petus of infinite Goodness by which, taking only
itself into account and leaving aside every other
consideration, it wills that all that which proceeds
from it be good and without any trace of evil.
But such a will may be frustrated.[6]

[5] That is to say, an inchoation which does not attain to being
an act of will, in other words a feeble movement by which one
does not *will* something but only *would will* it. When Saint Thomas
uses the word *velleitas* (*Sum. theol.,* I, 19, 6) it is in an altogether different sense and in order to signify a will which is
formal and properly so called but which is not unconditional nor
unfailingly carried out. Cf. John of Saint Thomas, *Cursus theol.,*
t. III, disp. 5, a. 7 and 8.

[6] Not, to be sure, in the sense in which a desire is frustrated
in us (by some exterior agent which deprives us despite ourselves
of what we will). The antecedent will is "frustrated," but by a
freedom that God himself has created, and which he has au-
thorized to evade him if it wishes, and which actually posits an evil
act only *with his permission.*

Let us note on the other hand that when by reason of an
ensemble of circumstances God has decreed something in view of
a good the accomplishment of which depends on our freedom—for
example that some sick person be cured so that he may repair an
injustice he has committed—the thing in question (the cure of the
sick person) occurs infallibly through the consequent will, but this

⤳ And from the very fact that there are creatures, it may be said that the antecedent will is going to find itself inevitably frustrated in a certain measure. For God plays fair with beings and means neither to constrain their natures nor to render these natures useless by substituting for them a constantly miraculous regime: there is no material world without destruction, and more particularly, from the moment that animal life appears, without suffering. There are no minds without freedom of option and (so long as they are not divinified by the vision of God) without the possibility of choosing evil instead of good. The possibility, inherent in our free will, of breaking by our "nihilatings" the divine motions which incline us toward good, has as its consequence that acts morally evil will be permitted whose first initiative—precisely insofar as they are evil—belongs to us alone. In this way our evasions and our refusals are in eternal eyes *circumstances* according to which, in the great struggle thus being waged, the consequent or circumstanced will, will accept for the antecedent will defeats that cause the saints to weep and will determine for it requitals and supercompensations such as brought the awestruck Saint Paul to his knees—both

---

will still remains for one part (in what concerns the future) antecedent and uncircumstanced. It could happen that this person does not repair and even aggravates the injustice he has committed.

the one and the other directed toward a final
triumph of that divine generosity all the more resplendent the more it will have been wounded
en route. ✍

★

God's will is adorable in all ways and under
all its aspects.

It is clear that by the third petition of the
Lord's Prayer the Christian soul asks at one and
the same time that there be accomplished the
voluntas signi, the consequent or circumstanced
will, and the antecedent or uncircumstanced will.
We believe, however, that the desire formulated
in this third petition refers principally to the antecedent will.

Nevertheless, it behooves us first to speak of
the consequent will.

The consequent or circumstanced will is always and infallibly accomplished. Why then ask
that it be done? That which has been decided
upon will happen in any case. Yes, undoubtedly;
but by this petition it is we who freely put ourselves in unison with this will and, whether in joy
or sorrow, bless its inscrutable designs: *dignum
et justum est, aequum et salutare.* . . . It is we
who in homage and thanksgiving, and by an act
of faith which can sometimes rend our hearts,

proclaim that all which our Father in heaven wills, whatever he may will to decree and whatever he may permit, is good because it is he who has willed it. "In saying: 'Thy will be done,' we rejoice that there is nothing evil in the will of God even if he deals sternly with us. . . ." [7]

To ask that the will of God be done—that is, his consequent or circumstanced will—is therefore sometimes a gift and abandonment of ourselves made in full agony. Perhaps it will be necessary to go so far even as to the sweating of blood. Jesus gave us the example.

After having first said: "My Father, if it be possible, let this cup pass away from me," he added: "Yet not as I will, but as thou wilt." [8] *Verumtamen non mea voluntas, sed tua fiat.* This prayer of Jesus is at the heart of all human sorrow and of all human hope. He had to die because he had taken upon himself all the sins and all the sufferings of the world—in consummation of his obedience and of the work he had come to do. It was before the absolute will, the consequent and definitive will of Him he loved more than his soul and his life, that he bowed his own human will and made abandon of it.

By the third petition of the Lord's Prayer we also pray for the accomplishment of the anteced-

---

[7] Tertullian, *De Oratione,* cap. 4, *P.L.* 1, 1158.
[8] Matt. 26:39; Luke 22:42.

ent will of God, the will which emanates primordially from his goodness but which can admit of obstacles. And indeed, as we have said, it is for the accomplishment of this antecedent will that we pray first and before all else. Why is this? It is because Jesus has us say: "Thy Will be done on earth *as it is in heaven.*"

Sicut in coelo—it is precisely this which we do not see carried out on earth. The will of God falls short of being done on earth as it is in heaven.

Sicut in coelo, that is to say, as it is accomplished by the holy angels and the elect, in the other world which is that of the vision of God and which will be that also of the resurrection of the body—there where free will, still in exercise as regards all that which is not God himself sovereignly loved, has become incapable of sinning—there where the angels by "myriads of myriads" cry out in loud voice: "Worthy is the Lamb who was slain to receive power and riches and wisdom and might and honor and glory and blessing," and in which every creature in the entire universe renders glory "to Him who sitteth upon the throne and to the Lamb." [9] "As the angels of heaven carry out thy will, Lord, may the same be done on earth." [10]

[9] Cf. Apoc. 5:11–13.—Cf. Ps. 103 (102): 21: *Ministri ejus, qui faciunt voluntatem ejus.*

[10] Saint Cyril of Jerusalem, *Catéchèses mystagogiques,* XIV, *P.G.,* 33, 1120.

By the third petition, writes Tertullian, "we ask that his will be done *in all men.*" [11] And Saint Cyprian: "Christ makes us pray *for the salvation of all men.*" [12] And Saint Augustine: "It is for *perfection* that we beg by this prayer," [13] And again: "Thy will be done *by men, even as by the angels.*" [14] And again: "So that his will may be done by us as it is done in heaven by his angels." [15]

As by the angels—in all men—for the salvation of all men—for the perfection of all men here below: it is clear that understood in the full force of *sicut in coelo* the third petition has as its first object, not the consequent or circumstanced will of God, which is always accomplished, but his primordial will. It refers first and principally to the antecedent will by which God wills that all men be saved, and that in creation there be found, in divers degrees, only good, without any sting of evil, neither evil in a relative sense or the evil of suffering, nor evil in an absolute sense, or the evil of sin. It is for the accomplishment of this will that Jesus taught us to pray first and above all, as it was for the accomplishment of this will that his own human will aspired of itself and above all.

---

[11] *De Oratione,* cap. 4, see above, p. 37, n. 28.
[12] *De Oratione Dominica,* n. 17, *P.L.,* 4, 530.
[13] *Serm.* 56, cap. 5, n. 8, *P.L.,* 34, 1278.
[14] ". . . *sicut ab angelis, ita ab hominibus.*"—*De Serm. Dom. in monte,* lib. II, cap. 6, *P.L.,* 34, 1278.
[15] "*Ut sic a nobis fiat voluntas ejus, quemadmodum fit in coelestibus ab Angelis ejus.*" *Ad Probam, P.L.,* 33, 502 (n. 21).

〜 This primordial and uncircumstanced will may be, if one may be permitted so to speak, outclassed, as when a certain good willed in things has as its reverse side suffering in them.[16]

It can also, as we have noted, be frustrated. It is in this sense that "God is wounded by our sin."[17] For "God does not do good in man if man does not will it,"[18] and man is able not to will it; he can evade the divine activation which inclines him toward good, and at the same stroke place an obstacle before the antecedent will.[19]

Sin is offense against God. But what exactly does this expression mean? What is its true sense, if not to signify that sin deprives the divine will— the primordial or antecedent will—of something it has really willed? "In his antecedent will, God wills that all men be saved, and he likewise wills that all my actions be good. If I sin, something that God has willed and loved will forever not be. This through my own first initiative. I am thus

---

[16] The evil of suffering is doubtless not willed directly and *per se;* it is nevertheless willed *per accidens,* or "allowed" by the consequent will.

[17] Charles Journet, *The Meaning of Evil* (New York: P. J. Kenedy & Sons, 1963), p. 182.

[18] Saint John Chrysostom, *Opus imperfectum, Hom.* 14, *sup. Matth.,* cap. 6 (Paris: Gaume, 1836), t. VI, p. 811: *Nam sicut homo non potest facere bonum, nisi habuerit adjutorium Dei: sic nec Deus bonum operatur in homine, nisi homo voluerit."* Cited in *Catena aurea,* in *Matth.* 6 (Turin: Marietti, 1953), t. I, p. 105.

[19] Cf. Saint Thomas, I *Sent.,* dist. 47, q. 1, a. 2, ad. 1. "Those who are not with God are, so far as in them lies, against God, from the fact that they go against God's antecedent will" (quoted by Monsignor Journet, *op. cit.,* p. 183).

the cause—the nihilating cause—of a privation with regard to God, a privation as to the term or effect willed (but in no way as to the good of God himself). . . . Sin not only deprives the universe of a thing that is good, it deprives God himself of something he conditionally but truly willed. . . . The moral fault affects the Uncreated in no way in Himself—He is absolutely invulnerable—but in the things and effects that He wills and loves. Here we could say that God is the most vulnerable of beings. No need of poisoned arrows, of cannons or machine-guns; an invisible movement in the heart of a free agent suffices to wound him, to deprive his antecedent will of something here below which he has wanted and loved from all eternity, and which will never be." [20]

*

How can we avoid touching at this point upon the question which the Heart of Jesus in glory afflicted by our desertions, and the tears of the Virgin who came down to our mountains to speak to two children do not permit us to evade?

Reason rebels at the idea of the conjunction of suffering and Beatitude. "The latter is absolute plenitude, and suffering is the cry of the

[20] Jacques Maritain, *Neuf leçons sur les notions premières de la philosophie morale,* pp. 175–6.

wounded. But our God is a crucified God; the beatitude of which he cannot be deprived did not prevent him from fearing or mourning, or from sweating blood in the unimaginable Agony, or from passing through the throes of death on the Cross, or from feeling abandoned." [21] It is by a suffering God that we have been redeemed.

It may further be remarked that "for a created being to be capable of suffering is a real perfection; it is the lot of life and of the spirit; it is the greatness of man. . . ."

It remains that "because the very idea of suffering implies some imperfection, it cannot be ascribed to the 'impenetrable Essence.' But in some form which no human can name, is it not needful that there be found in that Essence the whole element of mysterious perfection which pertains to the suffering of the creature?"

These inexpressible recesses of Light, "this kind of glory of suffering, perhaps it is to this that correspond on earth the suffering of the innocent, the tears of children, certain excesses of humiliation and misery which it is almost impossible for the heart to accept without being scandalized, and which, when the face of the enigmatic world has passed away, will appear at the summit of the Beatitudes." [22]

[21] Raïssa Maritain, *We Have Been Friends Together* (New York: Longmans, Green, 1942), p. 189.
[22] *We Have Been Friends Together*, p. 190.

The passages just cited are taken from *We Have Been Friends Together*. The author was careful there to excuse herself "for what is obscure in these reflections," and recalled with awe the famous words of Léon Bloy: "When one speaks lovingly of God, all human words are like blind lions searching for a spring in the desert." ✎

★

It is in the last of the first three petitions of the Lord's Prayer that there appears most manifestly the mysterious character which it has in common with the two others of being a prayer to God for God, a wish which the filial love of Christ and of his brothers addresses to God for God himself, for his triumph, for his eternal and infinite joy which desires to receive into it the intelligent creatures he has made. There is in this third petition a tenderness so ardent that it does not hesitate to go beyond the possible: *sicut in coelo et in terra,* "by men, even as by the angels."

"When the disciples asked Christ to teach them to pray, he gave them the Lord's Prayer, and the first three paradoxical petitions that they had to address to God," for "divine things" which "therefore will come about partially in dependence on our human initiatives. It must be concluded that the fervor with which God's friends

pray will decide, to a very great extent, the outpourings of God's helping graces, be they regular
or miraculous, the advances made by the City of
God, and any progress in the conversion of the
world." [23]

One might say that in passing from one stage
to the other the petition becomes more intimate
and goes in a deeper way to God's own good. May
honor and witness be rendered His holiness. May
His reign come to all men, and that kingdom
where His very divinity is participated in by created minds. May the superabounding Love which
is one with His Being, may the desire of His heart,
may His will find accomplishment without obstacle in the world of men as in the world of the
blessed in heaven.

The third petition is a prayer of loving ac-
ceptance, which means most often a prayer of
abandonment of self and of submission in the
midst of crushing trials and ruin, a prayer of pros-
tration in order to participate in the humiliation
of the Saviour. But it is also, and even more, a
prayer of exultation, of zeal and fiery desire, an
insatiable prayer, inflamed by love, a prayer
which makes us enter into the primeval desires of
God and of his incarnate Son, and which claims
for the glory of the Father that which will never
be fully realized here below and cannot be,[24] but

---

[23] Charles Journet, *The Meaning of Evil*, pp. 172–3.
[24] Cf. the *opusculum* of Saint Thomas Aquinas, *In Orationem*

which must be asked for with all the more fervor and perseverance and which will be accomplished at the end of ends in so much more beautiful a manner that every created mind among the saved will be in raptures with it.

Dominicam Expositio, in *Opuscula Theologica* (Turin: Marietti, 1954), t. II, n. 1068:
   "Such is the will of God, your sanctification (1 Thess. 4:3). This will of God cannot be perfectly fulfilled in the present life; it will be fulfilled on the day of the resurrection of the saints, when bodies will rise glorified and incorruptible."

Chapter III

THE LAST FOUR PETITIONS

4

GIVE US THIS DAY
OUR DAILY BREAD

After beseeching God for his glory, we beseech him for us sinners.

Why did not Jesus, who has told us to be perfect even as our heavenly Father is perfect,[1] include in the prayer that he has taught us a special petition relating to that perfection of love which is our highest goal here below, and which is set down as something each should tend toward in accordance with his condition and insofar as he is able. In truth this petition is not absent from

[1] Matt. 5:48.

the Lord's Prayer: it is included in the first three petitions, the ones addressed to the Father for himself. Because for those who wish to satisfy the Gospel precept to be perfect even as the Father is perfect, it is not their own perfection that they must ask for first, it is rather the Good of God, because they love God more than themselves and than their own perfection; it is not to their own perfection (to be attained) that they must attach the whole ardor of their desire—they are Christians, not Stoics—it is rather to the treasures of life and of goodness of their Beloved, who is Love and who asks for, and rejoices in, our love.

Those who are entering on the paths of the spirit should think a great deal about their perfection. Those who have advanced far enough on the paths of the spirit scarcely think any longer of their perfection—perhaps they have been too harassed on the way; in any case it is Another that they are interested in.[2] Christian perfection closes its eyes to itself, it has eyes only for Jesus and for his Father; it is not a perfection of impeccability but a perfection of love.

➤ Moreover, man's perfection is most cer-

[2] "They are no longer preoccupied with self, but only with the extension of the kingdom of God throughout the world that his Name may be loved by all men, beginning with themselves. All their prayers, petitions, works and sacrifices are directed principally toward this end and they are converted into invisible channels through which the graces of heaven descend on earth." Victorino Osende, *Fruits of Contemplation* (St. Louis: Herder, 1953), p. 310.

tainly the work both of God and of man together. It supposes on man's part a fervent and tenacious will, heroically patient and persevering. It supposes that man's liberty has, under God's grace, faithfully cooperated with grace. But if one speaks the language of practical experience and not of speculative science, and if one reflects that in the "sons of God, led by the Spirit of God," [3] the human will has always the second initiative, under the divine motion, but never the first initiative (it is of evil alone that we have the first initiative, an initiative of primary cause), [4] then, and in this sense, we must say that the perfect one, as such, derives everything from God, nothing from himself. What he draws from humanity is its weakness, and the proneness to sin always present in him; this is the lot of man the sinner.

This is why, when the petitions of the Lord's Prayer turn to man, it is to sinners that they turn —*non enim veni vocare justos, sed peccatores* ("I am not come to call the just, but sinners") [5]—it is with all us sinners, and according to our condition as sinners, that they are concerned (and who, indeed, recognize themselves to be sinners better than the saints themselves? "If we say that we have not sin," says Saint John, "we deceive ourselves,

[3] Rom. 8:14.
[4] "The first cause of the defect of grace is on our part." Saint Thomas, *Sum. theol.,* I–II, 112, 3 ad. 2.
[5] Matt. 9:13.

and the truth is not in us"[6]). The Lord's Prayer instructs, and while instructing us it puts ointment on our wounds. If there are some among us who think themselves perfect, they will be cured of their presumption. If there are some who would like to be saints and grieve because they are not, they will be cured of their sadness. If there are some who are plunged in evil and darkness, they will begin to have hope. ✍

What then do sinners need? To live, first of all, like the grass of the fields, and like those sparrows no one of which falls to the ground without God's consent. And to live as men, and as men redeemed.

And what they need after this is pardon, the remission of sins.

These are the two things they fundamentally need.

But still another thing is necessary for them.[7] For even pardoned they are still in danger; in danger because of weakness. They have need that God himself come to help them because of their weakness.

★

"Our *supersubstantial* bread, our *daily* bread."

[6] 1 John 1:8.

[7] It may be noted with Father Lagrange (*Evang. selon saint Luc,* p. 321, n.) that of the three things of which we are speaking the first concerns the present, the second the past, the third the future.

The same Greek word, ἐπιούσιον, is used by both Matthew (6:11) and Luke (11:3) to characterize the bread we ask for; but in the Latin version revised by Saint Jerome this same Greek word is translated in Saint Matthew by *supersubstantialem* and in Saint Luke by *quotidianum*. Truth to tell, the Greek word *epiousion* is an enigma, which already intrigued Origen, and concerning which modern scholars are scarcely more advanced than he. Origen remarks [8] that this word is not to be met with either in literary language or in popular speech; it was forged by the Gospel.

According to the etymologies consulted,[9] it means: in the first place, either the "bread of tomorrow," [10] or the "bread of the present day," [11] which is equivalent to the *quotidianus* of Saint Luke; in the second place,[12] either the "bread we need in order to subsist"—this is the meaning that modern scholars regard as the most acceptable [13]—or the bread "which is above our substance," because it is of the very substance of God (*hoc est, qui est de tua substantia* [14])—thus the *supersubstantialis* of Saint Matthew.

[8] *De Oratione*, 27, *P.G.*, 11, 509.
[9] Cf. Lagrange, *Evangile selon saint Luc*, p. 323, n. 3.
[10] If ἐπιούσιον comes from ἐπιέναι.
[11] If it comes from ἐπεῖναι.
[12] If it comes from ἐπί combined with οὐσία.
[13] Cf. Lagrange, *loc. cit.*—*Evangile selon saint Matthieu*, p. 130, n. 11.
[14] Saint Jerome, quoted by Lagrange, *Evangile selon saint Luc*, p. 323, n. 3, according to Dom Germain Morin, *Anecdota Maredsolana*, III, II, p. 262.

It appears in any case that the fourth petition of the Lord's Prayer can be understood in three different senses, which are moreover perfectly compatible: let us say, the univocal literal sense, the analogical literal sense, and the spiritual or mystical sense.

In the univocal literal sense, it is a question of material bread and of bodily food; we ask for that which we will need in order to subsist— *omnis sufficientia victus* (all sufficiency of food) as Saint Augustine says [15]—as much as is sufficient for each one, but above all for the poor. Jesus has pity on our poor flesh; that it may be sustained, temperately of course, yet sufficiently for us to escape from hunger and from destitution which, in the terrestrial order, is a kind of hell.

This is the first meaning of the fourth petition.

In the analogical literal sense, it is a question of the bread which is the food of the spirit: the truth and beauty of which every human soul has need, and above all the Word of God: "Not by bread alone shall men live, but by every word that cometh from the mouth of God." [16] We should always be hungry for every word that

---

[15] *Ad Probam.* Quoted freely by Saint Thomas, *Sum. theol.,* II–II, 83, 9.—Saint Augustine (*P.L.,* 33, 498, n. 12, and 499, n. 13) says: "sufficientia rerum necessariarum." Cf. col. 502, n. 21.

[16] Matt. 4:4.

comes from the mouth of God. And yet, taking into account our weakness and the ease with which we misuse even what is best, it is still as befits the poor that our petition is addressed to the Father: *sapere, sed sapere ad sobrietatem,* "not to be more wise than it behooveth to be wise, but to be wise unto sobriety." [17]

In the spiritual or mystical sense, it is a question of the bread that is Jesus himself: *Ego sum panis vitae*—"I am the bread of life. . . . I am the bread come down from heaven. If any one eat of this bread, he shall live for ever; and the bread which I will give is my flesh, for the life of the world." [18] One can scarcely see how the *supersubstantialis* of Saint Matthew could mean anything other than the Eucharistic bread. Also could Jesus, in the impulse of his love, think of the food on which man lives without thinking at the same time of the supreme gift of Himself which he came to bestow on us, of the Bread which is his Body?

We are told that this meaning, on which the Fathers liked to insist, departs from the proper meaning. [19] But if ἐπιούσιον means ἐπὶ τὴν οὐσίαν, "above the substance" (our substance is transformed by it, not it changed into our substance), it seems more correct to say that the spiritual

---

[17] Saint Paul, Rom. 12:3.
[18] John 6:35, 51.
[19] Lagrange, *Evang. selon saint Luc,* p. 323, n. 3.

sense of the fourth petition remains a proper meaning, although mystical or transcendent, and presupposing the first two meanings.[20] "Jesus," wrote Saint Cyprian, "is the bread of those who constitute his body." [21]

What would be, then, the most proper translation? To cover the first two meanings we believe we must translate, as is done in the Greek-Catholic rite: "Give us today our sufficiency of bread," or "the amount of bread necessary to us."

To cover the three meanings together, let us say with Theodore of Mopsuestia [22]: "Give us today the bread we need."

★

The fourth petition has us pray for today, not for tomorrow. "Be not anxious for the morrow; the morrow will have anxieties of its own. Sufficient for the day is the evil thereof." [23]

But we will pray tomorrow, and every day until our death, for what will be then our today.

★

In asking for our daily bread it is a kind of favor we are asking, a thing we are not certain

[20] On the three meanings distinguished here, cf. Thomas Aquinas, *In Orat. Domin. Expositio* (Marietti), n. 1078 and 1079.
[21] *De Oratione Dominica,* n. 18, *P.L.,* 4, 531.
[22] *Homélies catéchètiques,* Hom. 11, on the Lord's Prayer (Vatican City: Ed. Raymond Tonneau, 1949), par. 14, p. 309.
[23] Matt. 6:34.

of having for it is not assured us by nature. And if perchance it is assured us for today, we still ask for this favor as beggars and the indigent, for all those who do not have today what is sufficient.

That many do not have sufficient is all too true. And Jesus does not like this, nor does his Father. The remote cause of it is Adam's sin. But there are proximate causes; it seems that the responsibility of other men and of the great human community has a great share in the matter, at least by omission. If there were fewer wars, less craving to enslave or exploit others, fewer national egoisms, egoisms of caste or egoisms of class, if man cared more about his neighbor and really wished to bring together for the common good of the human species the resources which, especially in our day, he and his science have at their disposal and which he employs for mutual menace and destruction, there would be fewer peoples on earth who do not have enough bread and fewer children who die or are incurably debilitated by lack of food.

It is with great fear that we touch here on the mystery of universal solidarity. We ask ourselves, tremblingly, what barriers man in the course of his history (or must we still say his prehistory?) has raised and continues to raise against the Gospel. It has been said that to those who seek first the kingdom of God all else shall be added. Must we believe that as a consequence of conditions that more love and more justice could have prevented, there are men too bowed down by misfortune to have retained even the possibility of seeking first the kingdom of Heaven? Then will not this kingdom which they have not sought through no fault of theirs, in which through no fault of their own they have not hoped, will it not seek them out and await them at the door when they leave a world that has failed to perceive God's image in them? As for terrestrial history, it learns each day at its own expense that *Deus non irridetur*,[24] but it does not understand what it learns.

*

⤳ A minor question, which is a question of words, still remains to be examined. The message of the Gospel is addressed to all the peoples of the world. It is sometimes asked why Jesus used in the Lord's Prayer the word "bread" rather than a more general word such as "food," for example, since there are people who do not use bread and for whom rice or cassava or some other product of the earth is the most striking symbol of daily food.

Several answers can be given to this question. First of all, it is not abstract words like "food," but rather concrete, 'picture' words which

[24] "God is not mocked." Saint Paul, Gal. 6:7.

the Gospel prefers, and these words are inevitably particularized. It can next be noted that a certain particularization to a given historical and cultural milieu, that of the Jewish world at the time of Augustus and Tiberius, is implied by the very fact of the Incarnation, which took place at a given point in space and time; and this particularization due to concrete conditions in no way prejudices the universality of the Gospel message; it only needs to be explained, just as those to whom this message is transmitted need to be instructed.

Finally, Jesus had an altogether special reason to use the word "bread," if it is true that the fourth petition of the Lord's Prayer refers, according to one of the meanings it includes, to the sacrament of the Eucharist. And just as it is possible to procure no matter where a little wheat flour so as to be able to celebrate Mass, so also it is possible no matter where to teach the people one is evangelizing the meaning of the word "bread." There are, in particular for the primitive tribes (and also for certain highly civilized cultural areas), indispensable words much more difficult to translate and to explain than the word "bread." ✍

5

AND FORGIVE US OUR TRESPASSES
AS WE FORGIVE THOSE
WHO TRESPASS AGAINST US

Et dimitte nobis debita nostra. "Trespasses" or "debts," it is the same thing under two different names. In Saint Matthew (6:12) we read: "And forgive us our debts, as we also forgive our debtors"; and in Saint Luke (11:4): "And forgive us our sins, for we also forgive everyone who is indebted to us."

It is the good news of the remission of sins. What a marvel! It depends on us; a movement of our hearts (not easy, it is true, the most difficult perhaps for human nature) suffices for the Father in heaven to pardon the disappointments and wounds we have inflicted on his love. He has pledged it; in his name the Son has promised it to us. It is a fundamental law of the divine economy taught us by the Gospel. How God loves that we love one another! "It suffices that we pardon to have the assurance of divine pardon." [1] If I truly pardon there is no doubt that I shall be, that I am already pardoned.

This law was already recognized in the Old Testament, but imperfectly. If the texts of the Psalms [2] that Saint Augustine quotes [3] on this subject are not conclusive, Ecclesiasticus at least is very clear: "Forgive thy neighbor if he hath hurt thee: and then shall thy sins be forgiven unto thee when thou prayest. Man to man reserveth anger, and doth he seek remedy of God? He hath no mercy on a man like himself, and doth he entreat for his own sins?" [4] It must nevertheless be noted with Father Lagrange that "the idea of neighbor was ordinarily restricted to Israel" [5]; and besides, as soon as the idea of justice—of a justice still too harsh—intervened, the precept of compassion was counteracted by the law of retaliation; and the divine promise: you shall be forgiven if you forgive, had still not been explicitly made into the golden rule of the economy of salvation.

This golden rule was revealed to us in the Lord's Prayer. We are here at the heart of the Gospel. What is a Christian for peoples accustomed to the code of just vengeance and among

[1] M. J. Lagrange, *Evang. selon saint Matthieu,* p. 132, n. 14.
[2] Ps. 132 (131): 1; Ps. 7:4.
[3] *Ad Probam, P.L.,* 33, 503 (n. 22).
[4] Ecclesiasticus 28:2–4.
[5] Lagrange, *Evang. selon saint Matthieu,* p. 132, note.

whom the Gospel makes its first conquests? He is
a man who forgives.[6] "Ye have heard that it was
said, *'Eye for eye and tooth for tooth.'*[7] But I
tell you, not to resist the evildoer. . . . Ye have
heard that it was said, 'Thou shalt love thy
neighbor[8] and hate thine enemy. But I tell you,
love your enemies and pray for them that persecute you, that ye may become yourselves children of your Father who is in the heavens; for he
maketh his sun to shine upon the evil and the
good, and he raineth upon the just and the unjust."[9]

There is no other commentary on the fifth
petition than the Gospel itself. Immediately after
transmitting to us the text of the Lord's Prayer,
Saint Matthew's Gospel continues:[10] "For if ye
forgive men their transgressions, your heavenly
Father will likewise forgive you; but if ye forgive
not men their transgressions, neither will your
Father forgive you your transgressions." The
parallel passage is given in Mark in another
place, on the occasion of the parable of the
barren fig tree: "Whensoever ye stand at prayer,
forgive if ye have aught against anyone, that

[6] This is what Father Lebbe told us when he spoke to us of
his experience as a missionary in China.
[7] Exod. 21:24–25.
[8] Levit. 19:18.
[9] Matt. 5:38–39, 43–45.
[10] Matt. 6:14–15.

your Father who is in heaven may likewise forgive you your transgressions." [11]

He will forgive us our transgressions. Is this to say he will forgive the sins of those also whom we forgive? It was solely to the apostles and to their successors, not to the Christian people, that was given the power of the keys,[12] the sacramental power of forgiving sins. Those who have offended us and whom we pardon—how could God lag behind us and be less ready than we to pardon them? Nevertheless the grace efficacy, in their regard, of our pardon depends on their own free will and on divine mercy. This is why it is said in Proverbs,[13] in a text taken up again by Saint Paul: "If thine enemy hunger, feed him; if he thirst, give him to drink; for in so doing thou shalt heap coals of fire upon his head." [14]

Mysterious coals—not of anger certainly, otherwise how could Proverbs add: "And the Lord will reward thee," and Saint Paul: "Be not overcome by evil, but overcome evil by good"? These glowing coals burn with the terrible and sweet fire of the inscrutable divine will. In doing

[11] Mark 11:25–26.
[12] "Receive ye the Holy Spirit; whose sins ye shall forgive, they are forgiven them: whose sins ye shall retain, they are retained." John 20:22–23.
[13] Prov. 25:21–22.
[14] Rom. 12:20.

good to our enemies we entrust them to God, we call down on their heads the fire of the divine initiatives and attentions. If they resist the flames of grace they will fall, despite our wishes, into the flames of justice. But if they let themselves be won by grace and mend their ways and repent of their sins before God, they will receive the effect of the flames of mercy, in accordance with our wish, and the sins they have committed against us will be forgiven.

The fact thus remains that in forgiving those who have offended us we work in a certain (preparatory) manner and so far as we are able, to the end that in them evil be overcome by good and that they receive God's pardon; we contribute, to the extent that it is in us, to increase the sum of good on earth and to cause the work of the Prince of Peace to be accomplished there. ✍

*

If I truly pardon, we wrote above, there is no doubt that I shall be, that I am already pardoned.

But just the same, am I ever certain of having been pardoned? The question is to know whether I have pardoned *truly,* as it is to know whether I *truly* love God and my neighbor. And this only God knows with certain knowledge. God alone knows with certain knowledge whether I have pardoned *from the bottom of my heart,* as the Gospel enjoins me. At the end of the parable of the servant whose debt was forgiven him and who did not forgive the debt of his fellow workers, we read in Matthew: "Then his lord sent for him and saith to him, 'Thou wicked servant, all that debt I forgave thee because thou besoughtest me; shouldst not thou also have had pity on thy fellow-servant, even as myself had pity on thee?' And his lord, being angry, delivered him to the torturers until he should pay all that was owing. So also shall my heavenly Father do to you, if ye forgive not each his brother *from your hearts.*" [15] And what does Saint John say? "Little children, let us not love with word, neither with the tongue, but *in deed and truth.*" [16]

After all, if we do our best, why should we torment ourselves? To seek to know with certain intellectual knowledge, with proved and demonstrated knowledge, whether we really love and if we have really pardoned from the bottom of our heart, would be vain curiosity of mind and a grave error. For what God wants is that we turn away from ourselves and place all our care in him. He wants us to *hope* in him: then what we

[15] Matt. 18:32–35.
[16] 1 John 3:18.

cannot know with certain intellectual knowledge we can have a firmly assured confidence of —because of his own goodness and his will to help us, which are absolutely certain things.

It is in this sense that after having told us not to love with words, nor with the tongue, but in deed and truth, Saint John adds: "Hereby we shall know that we are of the truth, and before him we shall persuade our heart that if our heart condemn us, God is greater than our heart and knoweth all things." [17]

"If thy brother sin against thee, rebuke him; and if he repent, forgive him. And if he should sin against thee seven times in the day and seven times return to thee, saying, 'I repent,' thou shalt forgive him." [18]

Si poenitentiam egerit. Si septies in die conversus fuerit ad te, dicens: Poenitet me. This *si* is the condition presupposed by what theologians call "ordinary pardon" or "pardon necessary for salvation," as distinct from the "pardon proper to the perfect." If my brother, however gravely he may have offended me, asks me for forgiveness, I shall forgive him from the bottom of my heart. But if he does not come to me to ask forgiveness, I shall be ready to forgive him (*secundum praeparationem animae*), but without my necessarily

[17] 1 John 3:19–20.
[18] Luke 17:3–4.

having to anticipate him; and by the fact that I forgive all my enemies in general he will be included among them, but virtually, and without my having to accomplish for him in particular that act of *gift* through which justice no longer has any claim on him in my regard. "We must know that there are two kinds of pardon. One is proper to the perfect; in this case, according as it is said: 'Seek after peace and pursue it,'[19] the offended goes to meet the offender. The other is ordinary pardon, to which all are bound by precept, and by which we pardon him who asks us."[20]

We find the same doctrine in the *Summa theologica,* with regard to love for our enemies: "It is absolutely necessary, for the fulfillment of the precept, that we should inwardly love our enemies in general, but not individually, except as regards the mind being prepared to do so . . . it is not necessary for salvation that we show our enemies (such like) favors and signs of love, except as regards being ready in our minds, for instance to come to their assistance in

[19] Ps. 34:15 (33:15).
[20] Saint Thomas Aquinas, *In Orat. Domin. Expositio* (Marietti), n. 1091. Let us remember—but this is an altogether different question—that the perfect, like others, may have to exact the sanctions of justice against a guilty one in order to protect some superior interest of which they have the keeping. Besides, we are, even in such a case, bound in our person-to-person relations with the one we are having condemned, and as to that which in his misdemeanor has reached our own subjectivity, to pardon him in our heart at least *secundum praeparationem animae,* and, in case of necessity, effectively in action and by coming to his aid.

a case of urgency [21]. . . or if he should beg forgiveness. But to love one's enemies absolutely in
the individual, and to assist them, is an act of
perfection. In like manner it is a matter of
obligation that we should not exclude our enemies
from the general prayers which we offer up for
others; but it is a matter of perfection, and not of
obligation, to pray for them individually, except
in certain cases." [22] And again: "Charity does not
require that we should have a special movement
of love to every individual man, since this would
be impossible. Nevertheless charity does require
this, in respect of our being prepared in mind,
namely, that we should be ready to love our
enemies individually, if the necessity were to
occur. That man should actually do so, and love
his enemy for God's sake, without it being necessary for him to do so, belongs to the perfection
of charity." [23]

Such a doctrine is just and human; it pre-
vents us from loading souls down with burdens
they cannot yet carry, and from requiring of
others what we are perhaps incapable of ourselves. To truly forgive—not with the lips but
from the bottom of the heart—is a terribly

[21] Cf. *Summa theol.*, II–II, 25, 9. "Talia beneficia vel dilectionis
signa inimicis exhibere non est de necessitate salutis nisi secundum
praeparationem animae, ut scilicet subveniatur eis in articulo
necessitatis."
[22] *Summa theol.*, II–II, 83, 8.
[23] *Ibid.*, II–II, 25, 8.

serious thing; for even in "ordinary pardon" there is required preparation of soul, which supposes that we do not deliberately nourish within us, whatever may be the movements not consented to, any feeling of hatred against this or that enemy in particular [24]; and to forgive, be it only *secundum praeparationem animae,* is not only to renounce vengeance,[25] it is also to be ready to give the guilty one even that which he has taken from us, and thus to bring it about (at least in what concerns us, and also in what concerns our petitions to God) that he be henceforth in accord with divine justice and that he be released from its claims on him—he is liberated, his debt is forgiven. Forgiveness implies no detriment to justice; even in going beyond it, it seems that justice receives its due.[26] But it obliges (except when an interest superior to that of my resentment must be protected) that one renounce the sanctions that justice would have imposed. And for him who has not yet had his eyes washed enough by tears and his soul softened enough by charity, even this is felt—wrongly—to be a breach of justice. The poor heart is locked in

[24] "Whoso hateth his brother is a murderer, and ye know that no murderer hath eternal life abiding within him." 1 John 3:15.

[25] "The desire for vengeance removes from you all hope of obtaining pardon for your other sins," it "deprives you of any right to say: *as we forgive those who trespass against us.*" Saint Augustine, *Serm.* 57, *P.L.,* 39, 392.

[26] Cf. Thomas Aquinas, *Summa theol.,* I, 21, 3, ad. 2.

debate, it feels torn between two contradictory imperatives, it is in agony. An act of pardon required, in case of necessity, toward a miserable one who has destroyed or outraged that which a man holds most dear—it may be that this man will pay it with his life.

It remains that in case of necessity such an act of forgiveness is required by the Gospel. And it remains that the Gospel leaves to theologians the care of the distinction we have just mentioned between ordinary forgiveness and the forgiveness of the perfect. It is the *spirit of forgiveness* that the Gospel makes a duty for us; and the Gospel places itself less in the perspective of what is or is not prescribed as necessary for salvation than in that of the law of correspondence between the divine comportment and our own: pardon as He pardons; as thou hast pardoned, thou shalt be pardoned. Moreover, in the majority of concrete cases, it is not with my enemies in general but with this or that enemy in particular, whose dagger's blow I have just received, that my conscience has to do. Then, whatever I have against him, it is he in particular whom I must forgive in my heart and from the bottom of my heart if I wish to put my conscience at rest and to escape from an intolerable perplexity. My God, forgive me as I forgive him.

I am not, for all that, perfect. But when the Spirit blows, it carries beyond all limits traced beforehand; the spirit of forgiveness impels every Christian, perfect or imperfect, who wishes to obey the Gospel, to pass beyond the strict precept—if only for once, just for the turmoil I am in today. And ordinary pardon, which is (as we have noted above) more demanding than it appears to be, forces us in many cases to precipitate ourselves willy-nilly into the pardon of the perfect.

"But to you who give ear I say, love your enemies, do good to them that hate you, bless them that curse you, pray for them that mistreat you. To him that striketh thee on the cheek, offer the other also; and from him that taketh away thy cloak, withhold not thy tunic also. Give to everyone that asketh of thee, and from him that taketh away thy goods ask no return. In fine, as ye would that men should do unto you, so do ye unto them. If you love them that love you, what merit have ye? Even the sinners love those who love them. . . . And if ye lend to those from whom ye hope you receive back, what merit have ye? Even sinners lend unto sinners, in order that they may receive as much in return. Nay, love your enemies and do good to them, and lend without hope of recovery, and great shall be your reward, and ye shall be children of the Most High, for himself is good to the ungrateful and evil. Have pity, even as your Father hath pity. "Judge not, and ye shall not be judged;

condemn not, and ye shall not be condemned. Pardon, and ye shall be pardoned: give, and it shall be given to you: good measure, pressed down, shaken together, running over shall they pour into your lap. For with what measure ye measure, it shall be measured unto you in return." [27]

[27] Luke 6:27–38. (Cf. Matt. 5:38–48.)

6

AND LEAD US NOT
INTO TEMPTATION

Et ne nos inducas in tentationem. Καὶ μὴ εἰσενέγκῃς ἡμᾶς εἰς πειρασμόν. Two errors are to be avoided in meditating on the sixth petition. We must not imagine (as the literal translation, "And lead us not into temptation" might lead us to believe) that in order to test our resistance, God himself sometimes tempts us or incites us to evil. The interior troubles and dark invasions that the attraction of evil suddenly or insidiously produces in the soul arise from our weakness and our "own lust" [1]; they proceed also from the fallen Angel, who excites that lust and who, *tanquam leo rugiens,* "goeth about, seeking to devour." [2] It is the devil who tempts us, it is not God. "Let no man, when he is tempted, say that he is tempted

---

[1] James 1:14.
[2] 1 Peter 5:8.

by God. For God is not a tempter of evils, and he tempteth no man." [3]

"Say not: It is God who has made me sin: for he doth not what he hateth. Say not: He has caused me to err: for he hath no need of wicked men." [4] "Heaven preserve us from believing that God could tempt us." [5]

But from another standpoint we must be on guard against lessening or softening the meaning of Jesus' words. We must not imagine that we are told to ask to be dispensed from all that would make us pass through the fire of trial, and which by that very fact would imply some risk of our failing or sinning, which is the case with the majority of the occasions that human life has us encounter, and especially with every option in which it costs us something to choose for the good, and with every serious affliction, tribulation, visitation of misfortune or persecution, and more especially still with every temptation properly so called, and with those supreme temptations to which a soul agonizing on the cross is exposed. "Blessed is the man that is patient under temptation; for when he hath been proved, he shall receive the crown of life, which God hath promised to them that love him." [6] "But even if ye

[3] James 1:13.
[4] Ecclesiasticus 15:11–12.
[5] Tertullian, *De Oratione,* cap. 8, *P.L.,* 1, 1164.
[6] James 1:12.

suffer for justness' sake, blessed are ye." [7]

"As long as we are on earth, we are entangled in the flesh which struggles against the spirit, . . . we are therefore exposed to temptation. . . . Who could imagine men removed from temptations, when he knows how overwhelmed they are with them? Is there any moment when one is secure from having to struggle in order not to sin?" [8] "Does the Lord ask us to pray not to be tempted at all? Nevertheless it is said in the Scriptures: 'He that hath not been tried, what manner of things doth he know?' [9] And elsewhere: [10] 'Esteem it in all joy, my brethren, when you fall into various trials.' " [11]

Saint Thomas wrote the same: in the sixth petition "we do not ask not to be tempted, but not to be conquered by temptation." [12]

And what does the Apostle say? "All that will to live piously in Jesus Christ shall be persecuted." [13]

And what does the Lord Jesus say? "Blessed are ye when they shall reproach you, and persecute you, and speak all evil against you, lying, because of me; rejoice and exult, because your re-

[7] 1 Peter 4:15.
[8] Origen, *De Oratione,* 29 *P.G.,* 11, 532–3.
[9] Ecclesiasticus 34:11.
[10] James 1:2.
[11] Saint Cyril of Jerusalem, *Catéchèses mystagogiques,* XVII, *P.G.,* 33, 1121.
[12] *Sum. theol.,* II–II, 83, 9.
[13] Saint Paul, 2 Tim. 3:12.

ward is great in heaven. For thus did they persecute the apostles who were before you." [14]

*

A first point should therefore be noted. It is
that, as Father Lagrange reminds us,[15] the word
peirasmos means test or trial (everything that
calls on us to make proof of some virtue, especially of our fidelity and our love), and that
"test" or "trial" has a much broader meaning
than "temptation." Thus Jesus said to the
apostles: *Vos autem estis, qui permansistis mecum
in tentationibus meis.* Clearly the word *tentatio*
(πειρασμός) here signifies trial, and not temptation. "But ye are they who have remained with
me throughout my trials." [16] These trials "are the
difficulties of life, the ambushes of the Pharisees
and of Herod's men, the visible disapproval of
the religious leaders, despite their hypocritical
maneuvers." [17]

Likewise it is said of the just: "God hath
tried them, and found them worthy of himself.
As gold in the furnace he hath proved them, and
as a victim of a holocaust he hath received them.

[14] Matt. 5:11.
[15] M. J. Lagrange, *Evang. selon saint Luc,* p. 324, n. 4.—Cf.
Evang. selon saint Matthieu, pp. 130–1, n 13.
[16] Luke 22:28.
[17] Lagrange, *Evang. selon saint Luc,* p. 551, n. 28.

. . . On the day of his visit the just shall shine, and shall rush to and fro like sparks among the reeds." [18] And again: [19] "For thou hast tried us, O God: Thou hast tested us as silver is tested. Thou broughtest us into the net" (not the net of evil nor of temptation but the net of trial and misfortune).

And the supreme trial, that of Abraham, was not a temptation (an incitement to evil), but an order received directly from the All Holy God. "Was not Abraham found faithful in trial?" [20]

Nevertheless the word "trial" does not for all this exclude temptation; far from it—temptation is one of the most redoubtable forms of trial. It was not spared Joseph, son of Jacob; nor Job on his dung-heap; nor Jesus himself in the desert, nor any of His saints.

Another point to note is that of the kind of trial that is suffering, God is not the direct cause (*per se*), but is the indirect cause (*per accidens*); he allows it to exist because it is the reverse side of a good which he intends, or a condition or a means presupposed for that good. And of the

[18] Wisdom 3:5–7.

[19] Ps. 66 (65):10–11.

[20] 1 Mac. 2:52.—In the book of Tobias, the angel Raphael said to Tobit: "When thou wert burying the dead, leaving thy dinner untasted, so as to hide them all day in thy house, and at night give them funeral, I, all the while, was offering that prayer of thine to the Lord. Then, because thou hast won his favor, needs must that trials should come, and test thy worth." (Tob. 12:13— Knox translation.)

kind of trial which is temptation he is in no way
the cause, he simply permits it. Yet it is clear that
without his permission temptation would not
occur.[21]

"The adversary can do nothing against us
without the prior permission of God." [22]

⬱ This is why Saint Gregory the Great
wrote: "Men should know that the *will* of Satan
is always *unrighteous,* but that his *power* is never
unjust; of himself he exercises his will, but he
holds his power from the Lord. The iniquities he
proposes to permit, God allows in all justice." [23]
As Charles Journet adds: "No one, after God,
worked harder for Job's sanctity than the Devil,
and no one could have wanted it less." [24]

And what would we become, and what
would our misery be, if God did not have absolute
control over all the trials and all the temptations
that can assail us? Let Him slightly bow his
head, the trial will go no further, and the angels
of heaven will come to comfort and help the soul
in agony. And when thou art at the bottom of the
abyss, and he has rejected and abandoned thee,

---

[21] This is why Semitic thought, concerned above all with the
concrete event, paid little heed to the distinction between *to permit* and *to will.* Cf. Deut. 13:13, with regard to a trial which is a
temptation: "The Lord your God trieth you, that it may appear
whether you love him with all your heart, and with all your soul."

[22] Saint Cyprian, *De Orat. Domin.,* n. 25, *P.L.,* 4, 536.

[23] Saint Gregory the Great, *Moralium,* lib. II, in cap. 1 Job;
P.L., 75, 564.

[24] Charles Journet, *The Meaning of Evil,* p. 256.

and delivers thee to death and worse than death, he takes care of thy soul in secret, places flowers upon thy shroud and keeps the vultures away from thee. ✍

"Temptation hath not come upon you but such as man can bear; and God is faithful, and will not suffer you to be tempted beyond your strength, but will make with temptation an outlet, that ye may be able to bear it." [25]

Diligentibus Deum omnia cooperantur in bonum. "We know that for them that love God he worketh all things together unto good." [26]

The sixth petition is the prayer of our weakness, the prayer of a being who knows he is weak and prays not to be weak today, during the dangerous hours which will be the hours of this poor today.

It puts us on our guard against presumption. It is a prayer of humility (and humility does not know where to stop, though too there is no true humility which is not accompanied by magnanimity).

There is a kind of presumption which is only apparent, because it is merely a naive outburst of love and confidence. It is thus that the Psalmist asks to be tried: "Prove me, Lord, and test me: Try my reins and my heart." [27] And

[25] 1 Cor. 10:13.
[26] Rom. 8:28.
[27] Ps. 26 (25):2.

what should one say of James and John? Not only do they charge their mother to ask Jesus that they may sit at his right hand and at his left hand in his kingdom,[28] or in his glory [29] (to which Jesus answers: "Ye know not for what ye ask"), but when he questions them, "Can ye drink of the cup whereof I am about to drink?" they do not fear to say to him, *We can.*" Nevertheless the Lord did not reprove them for this, but said: "Of my cup indeed ye shall drink. . . ." [30]

But true presumption costs dear. Poor Peter! "Even if all shall be scandalized because of thee, I will never be scandalized. . . . Though I should have to die with thee, I will not deny thee." [31]

At the hour of supreme combat, we must pray not to enter into temptation; temptation would run too great a risk of exceeding our feeble forces. On reaching the Garden of Olives, Jesus "said to them, 'Pray that ye enter not into temptation.' " [32] And again when he found them sleeping in their sadness: "Simon, sleepest thou? Couldst thou not watch one hour? Watch and pray, lest ye enter into temptation." [33]

A man who truly knows his weakness will

[28] Matt. 20:21.
[29] Mark 10:37.
[30] Matt. 20:23.
[31] Matt. 26:33–35.
[32] Luke 22:40.
[33] Mark 14:38.

not refuse trial; he does not forget that in the midst of the worst afflictions and the worst temptations God will always help him. But it is himself that he mistrusts; he knows that a mere trifle is enough to lead him astray, that he is capable of every cowardice and every folly, of every lapse in grace.[34] Is he better than David, is he better than Simon Peter? Where they have fallen, will he be able to hold firm? And shall he be able to weep and rise again as they did? Lord, if you put me to the trial—with your help I will try to avoid every lapse, and if you will to go further, so be it, I will not try to escape. But will I cooperate with your grace? Will I not fall into the pit? Do you not realize my misery? Lord, do not put me to the test. . . .

★

∾ Here, we believe, in all their converging diversity and mutability, are the complex feelings of the soul to which the sixth petition corresponds. What words exactly translate the Greek text from which this petition comes down to us? This is not

[34] "We know that God tempers the wind to the shorn lamb. We must ask him, in his infinite goodness, not to allow us this day to come up against any temptation greater than our powers of resistance; or if he does, to strengthen us with a further granting of his grace. And also that he may not put us so greatly to the test as to expect from us all that he has a right to claim . . . and that he may take our weakness into account." Charles Journet, *The Meaning of Evil*, p. 238.

an easy question. Taking everything into account (and at least following the opinion of those best qualified to judge) it seems it is undoubtedly proper to give preference to the formula of the Hebrew translation: "And lead us not into the hands of trial."

The meaning of the sixth petition is in any case quite clear. It is the meaning which, by modifying slightly and fusing together a formula of Saint Ambrose [35] and another of Father Lagrange,[36] one could express thus: Do not allow us to be submitted to a trial or to a temptation we cannot bear; may thy Providence, always so ready to hear our prayer, never leave us exposed to occasions of sin too dangerous for our weakness. ✍

[35] "And do not allow us to be led into a temptation we cannot bear." *De Sacram.,* lib. VI, n. 29, *P.L.,* 16, 454.

[36] "May Thy Providence, always ready to hear our prayer, never forsake us in the snare of sinful occasions which threaten us in our weakness." *The Gospel of Jesus Christ,* vol. II, p. 16.

7

BUT DELIVER US FROM EVIL [1]

The seventh petition is "closely linked" to the sixth "in its form and in its meaning." [2] It answers it like an echo.

But at the same time it is "an ending that briefly sums up all the other petitions" [3]; in a single and final stroke it resumes them all, and with them the great prayer of the whole of creation. That is why it properly constitutes a distinct petition.

★

The Greek Fathers in general understood the word *ponèros* in the masculine (ὁ πονηρός), and said: "But deliver us from the Evil One." [4] According to Father Lagrange, it is

---

[1] 'Αλλὰ ῥῦσαι ἡμᾶς ἀπὸ τοῦ πονηροῦ.—Matt. 6:13.

[2] Lagrange, *Evang. selon saint Matthieu,* p. 131, n. 13.

[3] Saint Cyprian, *De Oratione Domin.* n. 27, *P.L.,* 4, 537.

[4] This version is adopted by the Jerusalem Bible (Paris: Editions du Cerf, 1956), p. 1296.

better to follow the Western tradition and understand this word as neuter (τὸ πονηρόν). In the Septuagint, where it appears often, it in fact signifies that which is bad or Evil, never the devil. In the same way Saint Paul writes: ῥύσεται με ὁ κύριος ἀπὸ παντὸς ἔργου πονηροῦ, "the Lord shall deliver me from every evil work (of my enemies)." [5] It is true that in a passage of Matthew [6] the word is taken in the masculine and signifies the devil. But that is the only passage in Matthew where this is the case.

This single case, however, seems to us slightly to shake Father Lagrange's position. For our part we think that the true sense of the seventh petition is indeed "Deliver us from evil" and that it does not directly refer to the devil, but nevertheless refers to him indirectly; so that in saying, "Deliver us from evil" we also say, although implicitly, "Deliver us from the Evil One." ✎

For the Prince of this world is the head of all the wicked,[7] and it was he who, when he tempted and overthrew Adam, brought down upon us Sin and Death and all the evils that afflict us, and he still claims to exert over us, in contest with Christ, what he holds to be his rights. When we ask to be delivered from evil, we

[5] 2 Tim. 4:18.
[6] Matt. 13:19.
[7] Saint Thomas Aquinas, *Sum. theol.,* III, 8, 7.

ask in the same words and at the same time to be delivered from his yoke and tyranny.

The evil from which we ask to be delivered is obviously moral evil, "every kind of moral evil" [8] to which temptation incites us.

Plato noted in an unforgettable manner that it is better to be punished (even and especially unjustly) than to be guilty. Moral evil, or "evil of sin" is, Saint Thomas taught, the pre-eminent evil or evil in the supreme sense.[9] Through it I escape from God to produce nothingness, I wound creative Love, and I crucify Christ. Through it, if I do not repent, I lose my soul. To say, "Deliver us from evil," is to say, "Deliver us from sin."

Nevertheless is there not another category of evil than the evil of sin? And must our prayer to be delivered from evil be limited to a given category of evil, even be it that of the preeminent evil? Our cry for deliverance has no more limits than Jesus' mercy. *Ab omni malo, libera nos, Domine. Ab omni peccato, libera nos, Domine. A fulgure et tempestate, a flagello terrae motus, a peste, fame et bello, a morte perpetua libera nos Domine.* Deliver us from all evil, Lord, from all sin first of all, but also from lightning and

---

[8] Lagrange, *loc. supra cit.*
[9] Cf. Saint Thomas, *Sum. theol.*, I, 48, 6.

tempests, from earthquakes, from pestilence, from famine and war, from everlasting death.

Deliver us from that unparalleled sorrow of seeing those we love suffer without remedy. Deliver us from spiritual darkness. Deliver us from anguish, which is doubtless the state of suffering on which the Holy Spirit has particular pity (is it not in such a compassionate mannner that it is always spoken of in Scripture?). Deliver us from the terrestrial hell of destitution. Deliver us from the tortures inflicted by men or by the cruelest maladies.

In second rank, certainly—because they are *evil* in a less radical and less formidable sense— the evil of suffering and the evil of pain are also included in the last petition of the Lord's Prayer.

This is what Saint Augustine thought when he wrote that it is the same thing to say *libera nos a malo* and to say with the Psalmist: "Deliver me from mine enemies, protect me from those who rise up against me." [10] No matter what tribulation the Christian may be suffering, Saint Augustine further explains, the last petition of the Lord's Prayer reminds him that he is made for that good in which one will no longer suffer any

[10] Qui dicit, *Erue me ab inimicis meis, Deus, et ab insurgentibus in me libera me* (Ps. 58:2), quid aliud dicit quam, *libera nos a malo?* Saint Augustine, *Ad Probam, P.L.,* 33, 503 (n. 22).

evil, and it likewise shows him the goal to which his groans and his tears should aspire.[11]

In the Middle Ages Saint Augustine's views were not allowed to fall into oblivion. "The Lord," we read apropos of the seventh petition in Saint Thomas' little work on the Lord's Prayer,[12] "teaches us to ask in general to be delivered from all evils, sins, infirmities, adversities, afflictions. . . . He delivers us from afflictions either by sparing us them, which is exceptional and concerns only those who are too weak—or by consoling us (If God did not console, no one could hold fast. We are 'utterly weighed down, beyond our strength,'[13] 'but he that comforteth the humble, even God, he comforteth us'[14])—or by

[11] "Cum dicimus, *Libera nos a malo,* nos admonemus cogitare, nondum nos esse in eo bono ubi nullum patiemur malum. Et hoc quidem ultimum quod in dominica oratione positum est, tam late patet, ut homo christianus in qualibet tribulatione constitutus in hoc gemitus edat, in hoc lacrymas fondat, hinc exordiatur, in hoc immoretur, ad hoc terminet orationem." *Ibid.,* cap. 11, n. 21, col. 502. We have kept the sense of this passage in abbreviating it. —Cf. *ibid.,* cap. 14, n. 26, col. 504: In his ergo tribulationibus quae possunt et prodesse et nocere, quid oremus, sicut oportet, nescimus; et tamen quia dura, quia molesta, quia contra sensum nostrae infirmitatis sunt, universali humana voluntate, ut a nobis haec auferantur, oramus."

[12] Saint Thomas invokes here the authority of Saint Augustine, but without giving a reference. It seems to us all the less doubtful that it is a question of the letter *Ad Probam* since one of the passages (cap. 11, n. 21) of this letter to which we refer above is cited in the *Catena aurea* in connection with the seventh petition of the Lord's Prayer.

[13] Saint Paul, 2 Cor. 1:8.

[14] *Ibid.,* 7:6.

granting us higher goods—or by changing the tribulation itself into good through patience [15]; the other virtues indeed avail themselves of good things; but patience turns evil to account, and it is in evils, that is, to say in adversities, that it is necessary." [16] ✍

The blood of Christ has delivered us from sin; but this deliverance will be fully accomplished, for each man, only at the end of his life—and this provided he has not refused grace. And at the same stroke we will be delivered from every evil of whatsoever kind. And on the day of the resurrection, when all will be consummated and Jesus will restore all things into the hands of his Father, the new heavens and the new earth will exult at being forever totally released from sin and from death, and from every tribulation and every affliction.

★

The last petition of the Lord's Prayer rejoins, so to speak, the first three. Like them it implies an ultimate eschatological meaning. Like them it will be fully accomplished only beyond this world and its history. It raises its protest against evil in all its amplitude and under all its

---

[15] Cf. Saint Paul, Rom. 5:3.
[16] In *Orat. Domin. Expositio* (Marietti), n. 1102 (condensed).

forms, against the root of evil, as against the
threat of evil hidden everywhere, and against the
empire of evil that locks the world in struggle—
against evil in all senses of the word, the final
defeat of which will mark the triumph of the
Holiness of God, of the Kingdom of God and of
the Will of God.

When we pronounce the seventh petition,
what passes through our lips is the deepest
aspiration of the very depth of the creature to be
supernaturally delivered from those very de-
ficiencies and failures whose possibility a universe
of created natures inevitably entails. And we do
not pray only for ourselves but for the whole of
creation, which "doth groan and travail . . .
while awaiting adoption, the redemption of our
body." [17]

The last petition of the Lord's Prayer has
not only a moral significance but also one that is
metaphysical and cosmic. Its reverberations are
infinite.

[17] Rom. 8:22–23.

Chapter IV

THE PRAYER OF JESUS

Who would dare, without trembling and without invoking graces from above, to lift his eyes toward what must have been those hours of unimaginable inner prayer when the Incarnate Word silenced all things within himself so that his soul might be free to experience lovingly, under the light of vision, the glory of his Father, of his own Divinity, and of the Holy Spirit? Theologians tell us that to the beatific vision, in which the divine essence causes itself to be grasped by the created intellect, there is joined in the blessed the experience of love due to the gifts of the Holy Spirit [1]; it is in this way that one

[1] Cf. Saint Thomas Aquinas, *Sum. theol.*, I–II, 68, 6.—In his

can think that when he entered into prayer superior to any concept Christ contemplated God, and called down divine mercy on men.

☙ And without doubt his contemplation also turned, in the tears of the gift of Knowledge, toward that poor humanity whose languors it was his mission to bear.

My God, enlighten a little for me this mystery, the thorns on the head of Christ and, within, his very bitter thoughts. Meditation for which "the representation of place" has been made by sinners on the body of the Blessed One, by flagellation and the other cruelties and the mock crowning, pending the Cross and Death.

On the Mount of Olives Jesus held before his eyes the subject of his prayer, all the sin to be assumed and the abandonment by men and God. Then began his agony in trembling and fright and the sweat of blood. And now, under the

---

treatise on *The Gifts of the Holy Ghost* (*Cursus theol.*, t. VI, disp. 18, a. 3, par. 77–79) trans. from the Latin by Dominic Hughes, O.P. (New York: Sheed & Ward, 1951), John of Saint Thomas writes: "The vision of God in heaven . . . is twofold" (p. 109). ". . . The light of glory elicits the beatific vision of God before there is any love, since it regulates and arouses love. The gifts of understanding and wisdom are knowledge founded upon and following after the love and taste of divine union with the soul and its being connaturalized with God through love" (p. 114); "From this vision comes love, and intimate affection and a fruition of God. From the fruition comes a loving and experiential knowledge both of God as He is in Himself—this the vision itself gives— and of God as He is attained and experienced within the soul" (p. 116).

*crown of thorns, he has in his humanity the vision
of all the evil that has been, that is present, and
that is to come.*

*Darknesses of the contemplation of sin,
truly implacable night, mystical and fathomless
night, experience founded in charity and in
Christ's union of love with sinners. It is for them
that he has come, to carry them on his shoulders
across the torrent of the ages to the solid land of
eternity.*

The King's bed is of wood of Lebanon, his
diadem is of thorns. *We have laid him on the
cross, all misery is naked before him, and his
bloodied head bows slightly upon his shoulder.
He tastes the infinite bitterness of our sins, as in
the darkness of divine contemplation the poor
saints taste the essential sweetness of God.*[2] ✍

★

When Jesus withdrew into solitude to pray,
it was doubtless first and principally to pray
without words.

But Jesus prayed also with his lips as with
his heart. He prayed aloud on Psalm Sunday,[3]
he prayed aloud in his great sacerdotal prayer at
the Last Supper, he prayed aloud in the Garden

---

[2] Raïssa Maritain, "La Couronne d'épines," fragment in
Lettre de Nuit, La Vie Donnée (Paris: Desclée de Brouwer, 1950).
[3] John 12:27–28.

of Olives, he prayed aloud on the Cross. And his vocal prayer of every day, is it not that very one which he taught us to say with him, after him? The Lord's Prayer is not only the prayer that Jesus taught us, it is the prayer of Jesus himself.

With what tenderness and longing he was to pronounce the great desires contained in the first three petitions! They were his own prayers which he offered to his Father, for the Name of his Father, for the Kingdom of his Father, for the Will of his Father; they were his own prayers before being the prayers which, as head of humanity, he offered in the name of his brothers.

The other petitions of the Lord's Prayer he pronounced in the name of the sinners that he had come to save, and according as, Mediator and Lamb promised to sacrifice, he was but one with those whose sins he had taken upon him.

So true it is that by essence the Lord's Prayer is a common prayer,[4] the prayer in which each of us addresses himself to God on behalf of his brothers as well as on his own behalf, the prayer in which the Son of God has pronounced not only petitions whose meaning held first for himself personally, but also petitions whose meaning held only for the sinners with whom he identified himself through love.

[4] Cf. Saint Cyprian, *De Orat. Domin.*, n. 8, *P.L.*, 4, 524.

It is clear that the last three petitions could not concern Jesus personally. He had no sins to be forgiven; he was not in danger of falling into temptation; he had no need to be delivered from evil—he, the conqueror of evil, the Saviour of the world.

The fourth petition, nevertheless, he made as we must make it, at once for the bread of which he and his had need each day while journeying on the earth, and for the bread of which the poor of the world have need every day.

And in a certain sense he could also make the sixth petition for himself, not through fear of sinning but through fear of having to endure that which revolts nature; and he could even make the seventh petition also, according as it concerns the evil of suffering. (*Pater, si possibile est, transeat a me calix iste.*)

To meditate each petition of the Lord's Prayer, trying to enter into the sentiments of Jesus himself when he pronounced it, would doubtless be a good manner of praying.

★

We have no other guide to eternal life, divine life, beatitude, than the Life of Christ, the Teaching of Christ, the Passion of Christ, and the Prayer of Christ. The imitation of Christ is the way of love and of holiness.

Thus the Lord's Prayer, taught us by Christ,[5] is the truest of prayers, the most completely and perfectly true, just and agreeable to God, the prayer whose flame must always burn within us.

There is no prayer, no contemplation, unless Christ be in the soul, and unless an imitation of Christ, a participation in his states and in his life, and in his prayer, what Saint Paul calls a reproduction of His image,[6] be present in the depths of the soul. He himself is also present there, because all the graces received by the soul reach it through the "instrument," "conjoined" to God, that is the humanity of the Saviour.

If it is a question of the particular goods, even the most justly desirable in themselves, for which, in the innumerable occasions of human life, we happen to ask God, but of which we do not know the role in the reverse side of things and the divine economy, we must believe Saint Paul: "We know not how we are to pray as we ought; but the Spirit Himself pleadeth in our behalf with unutterable groanings." [7] And what

---

[5] "Nobis formam orandi tradens, per quam maxime spes nostra in Deum erigitur, dum ab ipso Deo edocemur quid ad ipso petendum sit" ("To give us a form of prayer that raises our highest hopes to God, God himself taught us what we ought to request from him"). Saint Thomas Aquinas, *Compendium Theologiae*, II, cap. 3 (Marietti), n. 549.

[6] Rom. 8:29.

[7] *Ibid.*, 8:26.

then does the Spirit do? He makes us cry, "Abba! Father!" [8] What is this to say if not that the Spirit, when He makes us pray as we must, reminds us interiorly of the example of Jesus and has us pray, as "adopted sons," in the power of the Lord's Prayer? Every prayer in spirit and in truth, especially infused prayer in all its degrees, proceeds in the power of the Lord's Prayer.

Prayer without words is itself founded on the Word who is Christ. It is founded on the Prayer of Jesus. The soul formed by the Lord's Prayer prays—with or without words, in the murmur of words as in the bosom of the silence of pure contemplation—in the spiritual straightforwardness of the Lord's Prayer, in the imitation of Jesus.

In wordless contemplation the *Credo* is always there, in the depth of the soul. And one can say that it is in its light and its power that the soul passes to a knowledge or experience which proceeds from faith and from the union of love, and in which all concepts are silent (then the light of faith passes through them without awakening them, or while scarcely stirring them, so as to go toward the Reality which is its object, and which it makes the soul suffer through love, under the inspiration of the gifts of the Spirit).

[8] *Ibid.*, 8:15.

Likewise one could say that it is in the élan and the power of the Lord's Prayer that arise the desire, and the prayer, and the petition, however unformulated, which are immanent to wordless contemplation, in which they have no other voice than the breath of love. The seven petitions are always there, in the depths of the soul, but there is no longer need to articulate them in words; it is their spirit which the Spirit makes mount toward God.

If from the point of mystical experience it were possible, without interrupting that experience, to redescend toward words, it is the words of the Lord's Prayer that one would find at the base, since, to tell the truth, it is in starting from them, according as they are imprinted in the soul, that the soul has been elevated toward wordless union.

When the soul, to seek Him whom it loves,
   Having no guide nor light
   Save for the heart's ardent flame,
experiences the blessings of the night,
      O Night that was my guide!
      O Night fairer than dawn
      O happy Night which joined
      The lover to his bride . . .[9]

[9] Saint John of the Cross, *Canticles of the Soul* ("The Dark Night"), str. 3, 5.

then it is as if the petitions of the Lord's Prayer, or the one or the other of them, or even at times the first beginnings of some fulfillment, had let fall the weight of human formulas so as to be no longer anything but the respiration of love.

One sees thus that from the busy man who can only recite *Our Fathers* (but perhaps he has already passed under the regime of the Gifts, perhaps he is farther advanced than one might think in the life of the spirit) to the contemplative who is drawn with closed lips into union with God known as unknown, and who in those moments has no longer but a sigh of the heart with which to make the petitions taught by his Master, it is by a single and same way that all those go to God, whoever they may be, who in no matter what corner of the world hear the call of love and do their best to imitate Jesus.

★

≫ Saint Thomas recalls (but without accepting, it would seem, responsibility for it) [10] that according to Saint Augustine [11] there is a certain

[10] *Sum. theol.,* II–II, 83, 9, ad. 3. "Ad tertium dicendum quod Augustinus, in libro *De serm. Dom. in monte,* adaptat septem petitiones donis et beatitudinibus, dicens . . ." ("Augustine [*De serm. Dom. in monte*] adapts the seven petitions to the gifts and beatitudes. He says . . .").

[11] *De Serm. Domini in monte,* lib. II, cap. 11, *P.L.,* 34, 1286.

correspondence between the petitions of the
Lord's Prayer and the gifts of the Holy Spirit. To
the first petition would correspond the gift of Fear
of the Lord, to the second the gift of Piety, to the
third the gift of Knowledge; to the fourth, the gift
of Fortitude; to the fifth, the gift of Counsel; to
the sixth, the gift of Understanding; to the seventh,
the gift of Wisdom.

In a matter which after all is a matter of
opinion, and however unimportant one may be,
is it permitted, while retaining the principle, to
apply it differently than did the great Doctor of
Hippo?

It seems to us that this correspondence is
more satisfying for the mind if one establishes it
in the following manner [12]:

To say "Our Father who art in heaven, hallowed by Thy Name," this is particularly appropriate to the gift of Wisdom—and it is preeminently the prayer of the Peaceful, to whom it has
been promised that they shall be called the sons of
God.

To ask that His Kingdom come, this is particularly appropriate to the gift of Understanding—

---

[12] In this enumeration we depart partially from Saint Augustine (*loc. supra cit.*) in what concerns the correspondence between the Petitions of the Lord's Prayer and the Gifts of the
Holy Spirit. But we agree with him in what concerns the correspondence between the Gifts and the Beatitudes (Cf. *Sum.
theol.*, I–II, 69, 3, ad. 3; II–II, 8, 7; 9, 4; 45, 6; 52, 4; 121, 2;
139, 2).

and it is preeminently the prayer of the Pure of Heart, to whom it has been promised that they shall see God.

To ask that His Will be done on earth as it is in heaven, this is particularly appropriate to the gift of Knowledge—and it is preeminently the prayer of those who mourn, to whom it has been promised that they shall be comforted.

To ask that He give us today our daily bread, this is particularly appropriate to the gift of Fortitude—and it is preeminently the prayer of those who hunger and thirst for justice's sake, to whom it has been promised that they shall be filled.

To ask that He forgive us our trespasses as we forgive those who trespass against us, this is particularly appropriate to the gift of Counsel—and it is preeminently the prayer of the Merciful, to whom it has been promised that they shall obtain mercy.

To ask that He lead us not into temptation is particularly appropriate to the gift of Piety—and it is preeminently the prayer of the Meek, to whom it has been promised that they shall possess the earth.

To ask that He deliver us from evil, this is particularly appropriate to the gift of Fear—and it is preeminently the prayer of the Poor in Spirit, to whom it has been promised that the kingdom of heaven shall be theirs. ✒